The Family
Meal Planner

GoodFood

The Family Meal Planner

Thrifty recipes and 7-day meal plans
to help you save money and time

Edited by Helen Barker-Benfield

BBC
BOOKS

1 3 5 7 9 10 8 6 4 2

Published in 2009 by BBC Books, an imprint of Ebury Publishing.
A Random House Group Ltd Company

The Random House Group Ltd Reg. No. 954009

Addresses for companies within the Random House Group can be found at
www.randomhouse.co.uk

A CIP catalogue record for this book is available from the British Library

ISBN: 9781846077562

The Random House Group Limited supports The Forest Stewardship Council (FSC), the leading
international forest certification organisation. All our titles that are printed on Greenpeace approved
FSC certified paper carry the FSC logo. Our paper procurement policy can be found at
www.rbooks.co.uk/environment

Mixed Sources
Product group from well-managed
forests and other controlled sources
www.fsc.org Cert no. SGS-COC-005091
© 1996 Forest Stewardship Council
FSC

Commissioning editor: Muna Reyal
Project editor: Laura Higginson
Designer: Annette Peppis
Picture researcher: Gabby Harrington
Production controller: Bridget Fish

Colour origination by Altaimage, London
Printed and bound in England by Butler Tanner & Dennis Ltd

contents

Notes on the recipes

- Eggs are large in the UK and Australia and extra large in the US unless stated otherwise.
- Milk is semi-skimmed unless stated otherwise.
- Wash fresh produce before preparation.
- Recipes contain nutritional analyses for 'sugar', which means the total sugar content including all natural sugars in the ingredients, unless stated otherwise.

❄ Marks recipes that can be frozen.

Good Food are concerned about sustainable sourcing and animal welfare so, where possible, we use organic ingredients, humanely reared meats, free-range chickens and eggs and unrefined sugar.

Oven temperatures

Gas	°C	Fan °C	°F	Oven temp.
¼	110	90	225	Very cool
½	120	100	250	Very cool
1	140	120	275	Cool or slow
2	150	130	300	Cool or slow
3	160	140	325	Warm
4	180	160	350	Moderate
5	190	170	375	Moderately hot
6	200	180	400	Fairly hot
7	220	200	425	Hot
8	230	210	450	Very hot
9	240	220	475	Very hot

Approximate weight conversions

- All the recipes in this book list both metric and imperial measurements. Conversions are approximate. Follow one set of measurements only; do not mix the two.
- Cup measurements used by cooks in Australia and the US have not been listed here because they vary from ingredient to ingredient. Kitchen scales should be used to measure dry/solid ingredients.

Spoon measures

Spoon measurements are level unless otherwise specified.

- 1 teaspoon (tsp) = 5ml
- 1 tablespoon (tbsp) = 15ml
- 1 Australian tablespoon = 20ml

(cooks in Australia should measure 4 teaspoons where 1 tablespoon is specified in a recipe)

Approximate liquid conversions

metric	imperial	AUS	US
50ml	2fl oz	¼ cup	¼ cup
125ml	4fl oz	½ cup	½ cup
175ml	6fl oz	¾ cup	¾ cup
225ml	8fl oz	1 cup	1 cup
300ml	10fl oz/½ pint	½ pint	1¼ cups
450ml	16fl oz	2 cups	2 cups/1 pint
600ml	20fl oz/1 pint	1 pint	2½ cups
1 litre	35fl oz/1¾ pints	1¾ pints	1 quart

chapter 1

Batch meals and instant dinners

With a well-stocked freezer, you should never be stuck for something to eat. The dishes in this chapter require a little longer in the kitchen than many of the recipes in this book, so we suggest you prepare them at the weekend when you've got more time. Once you've made your batch meals and frozen half, however, what you're left with are ready meals at their best — healthy, cheap and homemade, so you'll know exactly what's in each preservative-free bite.

How to use this book

My grandmother had a large family to feed so, by necessity, she had to be a canny shopper. And, when her children grew up and took their children to visit, she could always make a roast stretch for a few more mouths. Even now, there seems to be an endless supply of rock cakes for anyone who drops by.

Once again, our priority is to save time, money and waste, but most of us have lost (or not been taught) the right culinary skills. Being a frugal cook doesn't mean you can't feed your family well or serve up good food for friends; it means planning meals properly, making a shopping list and learning to make meals stretch further or to make the most of leftovers.

For two decades, *Good Food* magazine has created recipes to show that home cooking is simple; that family meals on busy weeknights or more relaxed dinners for friends can be equally effortless; that you can cook delicious, balanced meals that are economical too.

Good Food: The Family Meal Planner is a collection of over 200 of *Good Food*'s most thrifty recipes. It's divided into five recipe chapters, each of which focuses on a different method of thrifty cooking.

Firstly, there are 'batch meals' that make two meals in one go. All these recipes feature freezing and reheating instructions so that you can make double the quantity, then freeze half to defrost and reheat later in the week for an 'instant dinner'. This way you'll save time as well as money – and avoid expensive, less healthy ready meals.

Next, there is a whole chapter devoted to the meals that many of us struggle with the most – finding something interesting and speedy to cook in the week. Along with each 'weekday supper' there's also a 'leftover idea' that uses either the remaining raw ingredients or the cooked surplus from the weekday supper as the base for a second meal.

In the third chapter, there are 'budget family dinners' that focus on simple recipes that use inexpensive ingredients but don't compromise on flavour. Consider this when you go shopping and don't get swayed by impulse buys, but have one eye firmly fixed on the bargains so that you know a good deal when you see one.

Some convenience foods make life easier – noodles in the cupboard will ensure you can whip up a meal in minutes, canned pulses are a cheap and healthy way to bulk out soups. Chapter 4 is full of ideas that make use of essential freezer and storecupboard ingredients, which last longer so can be bought in advance and kept on stand-by, ready to create a meal at a moment's notice. They are also often cheaper to buy than fresh.

Finally, there is a more indulgent chapter of 'weekend feasts' that includes plenty of three-course suggestions to try when you have a little more time to spend in the kitchen. These recipes are all great for entertaining. There are also some simple baking recipes and instructions for home-made stocks, which, if you have time to prepare them, are great thrifty cooking techniques.

Each chapter can be dipped into whenever you need inspiration as all the ideas work as stand alone recipes, but, if you use the meal planners in chapter 6, you can also sort out your shopping lists in advance and enjoy a thrifty recipe every night of the week.

Every recipe has been tested in the *Good Food* Test Kitchen, so that it will work first time for you and, where possible, we use full pots or packs of shop-bought items so you won't be left with half a pack or jar after making a recipe.

We hope this cookbook will inspire and help you to make the most of your money and time, and reduce your waste, but, most of all, we hope that we've chosen a collection of recipes that you'll enjoy cooking, and that you and your family and friends will love eating.

Helen Barker-Benfield
Good Food magazine

Batch cooking is clever cooking. There is great satisfaction in knowing that, after an hour or so in the kitchen, you can create enough food for at least two meals. You can save a significant amount of money by cooking in bulk too. Shops often offer better deals on larger packs, making them more economical. The problem is knowing how to use it all before it goes off – batch cooking is one answer.

Every recipe in this chapter serves at least four, but can be easily doubled or halved to accommodate the size of your family. To batch-cook these meals, double the quantities of all the ingredients then follow the green instructions for the 'instant dinner'. Enjoy half the dish straight away and keep the leftovers in the freezer to defrost and reheat later in the week or month when you're short on time – whenever you need an instant dinner. Most of the instant dinners in this chapter can be reheated or cooked straight from frozen, but if you plan a little in advance, you can cut the cooking time, and save energy, by taking the dish from the freezer the night before and allowing it to defrost in the fridge. Then all you need to do is follow the quick reheating instructions and prepare some rice or veg to serve.

Freezing know-how

■ Cooked meat and fish won't last as well as raw foods in the freezer, so try not to keep them longer than a month.

■ Wrap food carefully or put it in sealed freezer-proof containers.

■ Make sure you use a freezer-proof and ovenproof dish if you want to reheat cooked food from frozen.

■ Remember to write the name of the dish on the container and date it — it's easy to forget how long something has been lurking behind the fish fingers if it's not labelled!

■ An efficient freezer is a full one, as the air doesn't need to circulate as much, keeping running costs lower. If you've got lots of free space, you can fill freezer bags with stock (see chapter 5 for some homemade stock recipes) and stuff them into the holes, or stock up on essentials such as frozen peas and bread.

■ Cool cooked food as quickly as possible to avoid bacteria breeding. Don't put cooked food into the fridge if it's still warm.

Cooking from frozen

Some dishes, and many in this chapter, can be cooked straight from frozen. As a quick guide, foods that can be cooked from frozen include soups, stews, braises, casseroles and dishes like bolognese sauce, bakes, gratins and potato-topped pies, as well as thin fish fillets, small fish, sausages and burgers, and seafood too, if added at the end of a hot dish. Raw poultry and large joints of meat should never be cooked from frozen.

Chilli con carne ❄

This classic spicy dish is easy to make and ideal to have in the freezer for emergencies.

1　Put a deep frying pan on the hob over a medium heat. Add the oil and leave for 1–2 mins until hot. Add the onions and cook, stirring fairly frequently, for about 5 mins, or until the onions are soft and slightly translucent. Tip in the red pepper, garlic, chilli, paprika and cumin. Give it a good stir, then leave it to cook for another 5 mins, stirring occasionally.

2　Turn up the heat, add the meat to the pan and break it up with a spoon or spatula. Keep stirring and prodding for at least 5 mins until all the mince is in uniform mince-sized lumps and there are no more pink bits. Make sure you keep the heat hot enough for the meat to fry and become brown rather than just stew. If you are doubling the recipe, you will need to fry the meat in batches.

3　Crumble the stock cube into the hot water. Pour this into the pan with the mince mixture. Add the chopped tomatoes. Tip in the marjoram and the sugar, if using, and season with salt and pepper. Squirt in the tomato purée and stir the sauce well.

4　Bring the whole thing to the boil, give it a good stir, cover and turn down the heat until it is gently bubbling then leave for 20 mins. Stir occasionally to make sure the sauce doesn't catch on the bottom of the pan or isn't drying out. If it is, add a couple of tablespoons of water and make sure that the heat really is low enough. After simmering gently, the mince mixture should look thick, moist and juicy.

5　Drain and rinse the beans in a sieve and stir them into the chilli pot. Bring to the boil again, and gently bubble without the lid for another 10 mins, adding a little more water if it looks too dry. Taste a bit of the chilli and season to taste. Replace the lid, turn off the heat and leave your chilli to stand for 10 mins before serving with soured cream and boiled rice.

Per serving: 387 kcalories, protein 36g, carbohydrate 25g, fat 17g, saturated fat 6g, fibre 6g, added sugar 1g, salt 2.32g

Serves 4 ▪ prep 25 mins ▪ cook 35 mins, plus standing

1 large onion, chopped
1 red pepper, deseeded and
　chopped
1 tbsp sunflower oil
2 garlic cloves, chopped
1 heaped tsp hot chilli powder (or
　1 level tbsp if you have mild)
1 tsp paprika
1 tsp ground cumin
500g/1lb 2oz minced beef
1 beef stock cube
300ml/½ pint hot water
400g can chopped tomatoes
½ tsp dried marjoram
1 tsp sugar (see tip, below)
2 tbsp tomato purée
410g can red kidney beans

❋ **Instant dinner**
Make double, cool half and freeze in a freezer-proof container. To cook the chilli from frozen, gently reheat it on the hob, until it has completely defrosted and has bubbled away for at least 20 mins.

TIP Add a little sugar when using canned tomatoes to balance the acidity, or make your chilli a little special by omitting the sugar and using plain chocolate – a Mexican idea that will give the chilli a smooth, rounded flavour. Stir in a small piece (about the size of your thumb-nail) when you add the beans.

Spiced parsnip shepherd's pies ❄

These individual pies are ideal for storing in the freezer for those nights when you need a solo supper.

Serves 6 ▪ prep 30 mins ▪ cook 1 hour

for the meat sauce
2 tbsp sunflower oil
1 large onion, chopped
2 garlic cloves, crushed
small knob root ginger, peeled and grated
2 tbsp medium curry powder
500g/1lb 2oz minced lamb
400g can chopped tomatoes
100g/4oz frozen peas
for the topping
600g/1lb 5oz parsnips, peeled and chopped into large chunks
1 large potato, peeled and chopped into large chunks
1 green chilli, deseeded and chopped
large bunch fresh coriander leaves, chopped
2 tsp ground turmeric
juice 1 lemon
50g/2oz butter

1 For the sauce, heat the oil in a pan and add the onion. Cook until soft, add the garlic, ginger and curry powder, then cook until the spices release their aroma. Turn up the heat, add the mince and fry until browned, then add the tomatoes and simmer for 20 mins until thickened. A few mins before the end, add the peas.

2 Meanwhile, tip the parsnips and potatoes for the topping into a pan of cold water, bring to the boil, then cook for 10 mins. Drain, season and mash with the rest of the topping ingredients.

3 Heat oven to 220C/fan 200C/gas 7. To assemble the pies, place some meat sauce in six individual pie dishes (or one large dish) and top with mash. Ruffle up the tops with a fork, then bake for 20 mins until golden and bubbling.

Per serving: 424 kcalories, protein 22g, carbohydrate 27g, fat 26g, saturated fat 11g, fibre 8g, sugar 10g, salt 0.53g

❋ **Instant dinner**
Make double and freeze half the pies unbaked but assembled. Cook as above, but increase the cooking time by 20 mins, until the pies are piping hot throughout and bubbling.

TIP Clever shopping means thinking about the seasonality of the vegetables. Root vegetables are plentiful and cheaper in the winter, but peppers can cost a fortune then, so choose the dishes you want to cook when prices are lowest.

Veggie shepherd's pie with sweet potato mash ❄

The secret to this pie's filling is to use carrots that are big and old (in age rather than past their best!), so they don't lose their texture when cooked.

1 Heat the oil in a frying pan, then fry the onion until golden. Add the carrots and all but a sprinkling of the thyme. Pour in the wine, 150ml of water and the tomatoes, then sprinkle in the stock cubes and simmer for 10 mins. Tip in the can of lentils, including their juice, then cover and simmer for another 10 mins until the carrots still have a bit of bite and the lentils are pulpy.

2 Meanwhile, boil the sweet potatoes for 15 mins until tender, drain well, then mash with the butter and season to taste. Pile the lentil mixture into a pie dish, spoon the mash on top, then sprinkle over the cheese and remaining thyme.

3 Heat oven to 190C/fan 170C/gas 5. Cook for 20 mins if cooking straight away, or for 40 mins from chilled, until golden and hot all the way through.

Per serving: 531 kcalories, protein 16g, carbohydrate 79g, fat 17g, saturated fat 8g, fibre 12g, sugar 31g, salt 3.95g

❄ **Instant dinner**
Make double and freeze half uncooked but assembled, then defrost and bake as above. If cooking from frozen, heat oven to 160C/fan 140C/gas 3 for 20 mins, then turn up the oven to 190C/fan 170C/gas 5 for the rest of the cooking time.

Serves 4 ▪ prep 25 mins ▪ cook 20 mins

1 tbsp olive oil
1 large onion, chopped
2 large carrots (500g/1lb 2oz in total), cut into sugar-cube size pieces
2 tbsp fresh thyme leaves
200ml/8fl oz red wine
400g can chopped tomatoes
2 vegetable stock cubes
410g can green lentils
950g/2lb 2oz sweet potatoes, peeled and chopped
25g/1oz butter
85g/3oz mature vegetarian cheddar, grated

Pan-fried chicken in mushroom sauce ❋

This is such an aromatic and attractive dish that you should serve it straight from the casserole with the lid on for maximum impact.

Serves 6 ■ prep 30 mins ■ cook 1–1¼ hours

2 tbsp sunflower oil
6 large chicken legs, skin on, halved at the joint to make 6 thighs and 6 drumsticks
700ml/1¼ pints chicken stock (or water)
50g/2oz butter
1 onion, finely chopped
400g/14oz mixed wild mushrooms or chestnut mushrooms
300ml/½ pint dry white wine
300ml/½ pint double cream

1   Heat the oil in a large non-stick frying pan. Fry the thighs for 8–10 mins, skin-side only, until golden brown, then transfer to a flameproof casserole dish. Fry the drumsticks for about 5 mins each side and add them to the thighs.

2   Pour the stock over the chicken. There should be enough stock just to cover the chicken, if not add a little water. Bring the stock to the boil and cover, leaving the lid slightly off. Cook at just below simmering point for 30–35 mins until the chicken is cooked.

3   While the chicken is simmering, drain the oil from the pan. Heat the butter in the pan and add the onion. Sweat for 5 mins until soft but not coloured. Turn up the heat, add the mushrooms, then fry for 3 mins until they soften and start to smell wonderful. Pour over the white wine, raise the heat to maximum and boil rapidly for 6–8 mins until reduced by two-thirds.

4   Strain the stock into a pan with the onion, mushrooms and white wine, bring back to the boil and reduce again by two-thirds until it is thick and syrupy. Pour in the double cream, bring to the boil, season if you want, then pour the sauce over the chicken. Heat the chicken through in the sauce for 2–3 mins then turn off the heat and leave for a few mins before serving.

Per serving: 600 kcalories, protein 50g, carbohydrate 3g, fat 40g, saturated fat 22g, fibre 1g, added sugar none, salt 0.8g

❋   **Instant dinner**
Make double, cool half and freeze after step 3 until ready to use. Defrost thoroughly and then follow the recipe from step 4. Simmer the chicken in the sauce for 20 mins until it is piping hot throughout and the sauce is bubbling.

Five-a-day tagine ❄

This freezer-friendly Moroccan-style stew contains all of your five-a-day veg. Serve with a mound of warm couscous for a colourful and moreish meal.

Serves 4 ■ prep 10 mins ■ cook 35 mins

4 carrots, chopped
4 small or 3 large parsnips, chopped
3 red onions, cut into wedges
2 red peppers, deseeded and chopped
2 tbsp olive oil
1 tsp each ground cumin, paprika, cinnamon and mild chilli powder
400g can chopped tomatoes
2 small handfuls soft dried apricots
2 tsp honey

1   Heat oven to 200C/fan 180C/gas 6. Scatter the veg over a couple of baking sheets, drizzle with half the oil, season, then rub the oil over the veg with your hands to coat. Roast for 30 mins until tender and beginning to brown.

2   Meanwhile, fry the spices in the remaining oil for 1 min – they should sizzle and start to smell aromatic. Tip in the tomatoes, apricots, honey and a can of water. Simmer for 5 mins until the sauce is slightly reduced and the apricots plump, then stir in the veg and some seasoning. Serve with couscous or jacket potatoes.

Per serving: 272 kcalories, protein 7g, carbohydrate 45g, fat 8g, saturated fat 1g, fibre 12g, sugar 32g, salt 0.35g

❄   **Instant dinner**
Make double, cool half and freeze for up to 2 months. Defrost the dish then transfer to a pan, bring to the boil and simmer until the veg is piping hot but not completely falling apart.

Spicy root and lentil casserole ❄

Potatoes complement spicy flavours beautifully and are especially good in this simple veggie curry.

1   Heat the oil in a large pan, add the onion and garlic and cook over a medium heat for 3–4 mins until softened, stirring occasionally. Tip in the potatoes, carrots and parsnips, turn up the heat and cook for 6–7 mins, stirring, until the vegetables are golden.

2   Stir in the curry paste or powder, pour in the stock and bring to the boil. Reduce the heat, add the lentils, cover and simmer for 15–20 mins until the lentils and vegetables are tender and the sauce has thickened.

3   Stir in most of the coriander, season and heat for a minute or so. Top with yogurt and the rest of the coriander. Serve with naan bread.

Per serving: 378 kcalories, protein 14g, carbohydrate 64g, fat 9g, saturated fat 1g, fibre 10g, added sugar none, salt 1.24g

❄ **Instant dinner**
Make double, following the method to the end of step 2. Halve and do not add the coriander and the yogurt to the instant dinner portion, cool and freeze. To defrost, transfer to a pan and gently bring to the boil, then simmer until hot and bubbling. Add the coriander to the pan then serve, as above, with the yogurt and naan bread.

Serves 4 ▪ prep 10–15 mins ▪ cook 25–30 mins

2 tbsp sunflower oil
1 onion, chopped
2 garlic cloves, crushed
700g/1lb 9oz potatoes, peeled
    and chopped
4 carrots, thickly sliced
2 parsnips, thickly sliced
2 tbsp curry paste or powder
1 litre/1¾ pints vegetable stock
100g/4oz red split lentils
small bunch fresh coriander
    leaves, roughly chopped

Spiced lamb with chickpeas ❄

A no-fuss, yet satisfying supper with a gentle kick.

**Serves 4 ■ prep 5 mins
■ cook 1½ hours**

700g/1lb 9oz cubed lamb
400g can tomatoes
2–3 tsp harissa paste
410g can chickpeas, drained
handful fresh coriander leaves,
    chopped

1 Rinse the lamb and pat dry with kitchen paper. Tip into a large pan and add tomatoes. Half fill the tomato can with water and add to the lamb with the harissa paste and a good sprinkling of salt and pepper.

2 Bring the liquid to the boil, then reduce the heat, cover and simmer for 1—1¼ hours, until the lamb is tender. Rinse the chickpeas and add them to the pan, then simmer for a further 5 mins.

3 Taste and add more seasoning if necessary. Scatter over the chopped coriander leaves and serve with couscous or rice.

Per serving: 410 kcalories, protein 40g, carbohydrate 13g, fat 22g, saturated fat 9g, fibre 4g, added sugar none, salt 0.91g

❄ **Instant dinner**
Make double, cool half and do not add the chickpeas and herbs to the instant dinner portion then freeze. Defrost and bring back to the boil. Simmer for 30 mins or until the lamb is piping hot, adding the chickpeas for the last 5 mins of cooking. Finish with a scattering of herbs.

Vegetarian lasagne ❄

This light lasagne, packed with vegetables, is topped with a quick crème fraîche sauce.

Serves 4 ▪ prep 15 mins ▪ cook 1 hour

2 tbsp olive oil
1 onion, chopped
1 garlic clove, chopped
1 aubergine, cut into chunks
1 red pepper, deseeded and chopped
8 plum tomatoes, halved
350ml/12fl oz passata
200g/8oz ready-cooked lasagne sheets
6 tbsp crème fraîche
2 tbsp grated parmesan

1 Heat oven to 190C/fan 170C/gas 5. Toss the first 6 ingredients together and roast in a large, shallow tin for 35 mins until lightly charred. Spoon a layer of roasted veg over the bottom of a medium ovenproof baking dish.

2 Pour over some passata and cover with a layer of lasagne sheets. Repeat layers to use up all the roasted veg and passata, finishing with a layer of lasagne. Use a spoon to dollop over the crème fraîche, then sprinkle with the parmesan. Return to the oven for 25 mins, until the lasagne is heated through and the top is golden and bubbling.

Per serving: 404 kcalories, protein 11.4g, carbohydrate 53.3g, fat 17.6g, saturated fat 7.3g, fibre 6.4g, sugar 15.2g, salt 0.60g

❄ **Instant dinner**
Make double and assemble two lasagnes. Cool one and freeze before baking. Defrost thoroughly, then cook as above. You may need to increase the cooking time by 10 mins, but check after 25 mins.

Roast vegetable cassoulet ❄

This adaptable dish works with any veg that roasts well. Try parsnips or swede, even sweet potato. Look for what's in season.

Serves 6 ■ prep 1½ hours, plus 2 hours soaking for the beans ■ cook 50 mins

350g/12oz dried haricot beans
bundle fresh thyme, bay leaves
    and parsley stalks, tied together
    with fine string
3 medium onions, 1 quartered,
    2 chopped
450g/1lb carrots, 2 quartered,
    rest chopped
175ml/6fl oz olive oil
2 celery sticks, chopped
4 garlic cloves, chopped
400g can chopped tomatoes
1 tsp light muscovado sugar
4 tsp fresh tarragon, chopped
1 medium butternut squash,
    peeled, deseeded and chopped
1 medium celeriac, peeled and
    chopped
1 tbsp Dijon mustard
4 tbsp fresh parsley leaves,
    chopped
85g/3oz fresh white breadcrumbs

1 Bring the beans to the boil in a pan of cold water, simmer for 5 mins, take off the heat and cover tightly. Leave for 2 hours.

2 Drain the beans, return to the pan, cover with fresh cold water and add the herb bundle and the quartered vegetables. Bring to the boil and simmer for 1 hour until tender.

3 Heat oven to 200C/fan 180C/gas 6. Heat 3 tbsp of the oil in a flameproof casserole dish and fry the chopped onion and celery until soft. Add the garlic and cook for 3—4 mins. Stir in the tomatoes, sugar and half the tarragon. Season with salt and pepper.

4 Drain the beans, reserving 1.2 litres of liquid. Discard the quartered veg and herbs. Stir 600ml of the liquid into the tomato mixture and simmer, half-covered, for 30 mins. Toss the squash, carrot and celeriac chunks in 5 tbsp oil. Tip into a roasting tin and cook for 30 mins.

5 Remove the vegetables and reduce the heat to 180C/fan 160C/gas 4. Stir the beans, vegetables, mustard and half the parsley into the casserole. Add liquid if needed to make the mixture nicely moist. Check seasoning. Turn into a wide baking dish. (You can prepare to this stage the day before. Cool, cover and chill. Next day, if the beans have absorbed too much liquid, add more bean liquid or stock.)

6 Mix the breadcrumbs with the remaining parsley and tarragon. Scatter over and drizzle with the remaining oil. Bake for 50 mins. Serve from the dish.

Per serving: 486 kcalories, protein 18g, carbohydrate 57g, fat 22g, saturated fat 3g, fibre 16g, added sugar 1g, salt 0.86g

❄ **Instant dinner**
Make double and, at the end of step 5, cool half then freeze the mixture and store in the freezer in an ovenproof dish. Make up the breadcrumbs and freeze in a bag. When ready to reheat, heat oven to 180C/fan 160C/gas 4. Sprinkle the frozen breadcrumbs over the top of the dish and bake for 50—60 mins, until the mixture is hot and bubbling.

Asian pork and aubergine hotpot ❄

Slow-cooked aubergines become meltingly soft and happily absorb all the flavour of the stew juices.

1　Heat oven to 200C/fan 180C/gas 6. Heat 2 tbsp of the oil in an ovenproof pan and brown the meat well (you may have to do this in batches), then scoop out of the pan. Add the rest of the oil and the aubergine, brown on all sides, scoop out and add to the pork. Tip the sugar into the pan and leave to caramelize slightly. Return the pork and aubergine to the pan with the star anise and cinnamon then coat in the sticky caramel.

2　Add the onions, ginger and half the chilli, and cook for a few mins with the pork. Add the coriander stalks and splash in the fish sauce and enough water to come about a third of the way up. Cover and put the dish, undisturbed, in the oven for 1 hour, then remove from the oven and add the lime juice and more fish sauce, to taste.

3　Stir through the remaining chilli and half the coriander leaves. Serve scattered with the remaining coriander.

Per serving: 574 kcalories, protein 38g, carbohydrate 18g, fat 40g, saturated fat 13g, fibre 4g, sugar 15g, salt 1.81g

Serves 4 ▪ prep 20 mins ▪ cook 1 hour 20 mins

3 tbsp sunflower oil
750g/1lb 10oz fatty pork, such as shoulder or skinless belly, cut into large chunks
2 aubergines, chopped
2 tbsp dark muscovado sugar
5 star anise
1 cinnamon stick
2 onions, chopped
very large knob root ginger, peeled and finely chopped
1 red chilli, deseeded and chopped
bunch fresh coriander, leaves and stalks separated, stalks finely chopped
2 tbsp fish sauce
juice 1 large lime

❄　**Instant dinner**
Make double following the method to the end of step 2. Cool half but do not add the coriander and remaining chilli then freeze. When ready to use, defrost and heat gently to boil, simmer until piping hot and bubbling then add the coriander leaves and the rest of the chilli.

Multi mince ❄

Use this as a great base in one of the recipes that follows or freeze a batch ready to whip out for last-minute dinners.

Serves 8 ■ prep 10 mins ■ cook 1 hour

2 tbsp olive oil
1kg/2lb 4oz minced beef
2 bacon rashers, chopped
2 onions, finely chopped
2 garlic cloves, finely chopped
150ml/¼ pint red wine
500ml/18fl oz beef stock
leaves from 3 fresh thyme sprigs

TIP Lean mince often tends to be expensive. As you're frying the beef first in this recipe it's fine to buy ordinary mince as you can drain away any excess fat once it's browned.

1 Heat the olive oil in a non-stick frying pan. When hot, tip in the mince and cook for 10 mins until browned all over, breaking up any lumps with the back of a spoon. Tip on to a plate (you may need to do this in batches).

2 Add the bacon to the pan with the onion and garlic, then cook for 7 mins until the bacon is cooked and onion softened. Return the mince to the pan, then pour in the red wine, stock and thyme leaves. Bring to a boil then simmer for 30 mins until the mince is tender and the sauce has reduced down.

Per serving: 227 kcalories, protein 30.4g, carbohydrate 3.9g, fat 9.4g, saturated fat 3g, fibre 0.5g, sugar 2.7g, salt 0.70g

❄ **Instant dinner**
Make double the quantity you need, cool half and freeze to make one of the two following recipes. You can divide the mince into smaller batches before freezing. It will keep for up to 1 month. To use, tip into a pan with a splash of water, heat gently until defrosted then bring to the boil and simmer for 15 mins or until piping hot.

Spaghetti bolognese ❄

This will make a quick midweek meal if you have a batch in the freezer. Serve with any pasta, and the sauce will cling to it nicely.

Serves 4 ■ prep 10 mins ■ cook 30 mins

1 quantity Multi mince
350g/12oz spaghetti
grated parmesan, to serve

❄ **Instant dinner**
The spaghetti won't freeze but the Multi mince will, as long as it has not already been frozen.

1 Tip the frozen Multi mince into a pan with a splash of water. Gently bring to the boil then simmer for about 20 mins or until the mixture has defrosted and is bubbling.

2 While the mince is simmering, cook the spaghetti according to the pack instructions. Drain and divide among four warmed bowls. Top with the mince and serve with grated parmesan.

Per serving: 527 kcalories, protein 40.9g, carbohydrate 68.8g, fat 11g, saturated fat 3.2g, fibre 3g, sugar 5.6g, salt 0.70g

Rösti bolognese bake ❄

This continental version of a classic cottage pie is a great way to use the Multi mince recipe opposite. You can add more vegetables to the mix if you like. Chop finely or grate them, then add to the mince mix when you're heating it up.

1 Boil the potatoes for about 15 mins until tender. Drain and leave to cool. Heat the Multi mince with the red pepper sauce until hot and bubbling.

2 Heat oven to 200C/fan 180C/gas 6. Peel the potatoes and grate them into a bowl. Add the oil and three-quarters of the cheese, season and mix lightly.

3 Spoon the beef into an ovenproof dish. Scatter over the rösti topping and sprinkle over the rest of the cheese. Bake for 45 mins until bubbling and golden.

Per serving: 509 kcalories, protein 38.8g, carbohydrate 40.5g, fat 21.8g, saturated fat 6.9g, fibre 3.8g, sugar 9.7g, salt 1.85g

Serves 4 ■ prep 15 mins ■ cook 1 hour

700g/1lb 9oz potatoes
1 quantity Multi mince
350g jar sweet red pepper sauce
1 tbsp olive oil
50g/2oz mature cheddar, grated

❄ **Instant dinner**
This can be frozen as long as the Multi mince hasn't been frozen before. Make double and freeze half, uncooked but assembled. Defrost the dish and heat the oven as stated above, then bake for 45 mins until bubbling. Alternatively, if cooking from frozen, start the oven at 160C/fan 140C/gas 3 for the first 20 mins then increase the heat and continue baking.

Butternut squash casserole ❄

Pumpkin also works well in this recipe, so choose whichever is the best price.

Serves 4 ■ prep 20 mins ■ cook 40 mins

2 tbsp olive oil
1 onion, chopped
2 garlic cloves, crushed
1 tsp cumin seeds
1 tbsp paprika
200g/8oz sweet potatoes, cubed
1 red pepper, deseeded and
　chopped
1 butternut squash (about
　550g/1lb 4oz), peeled and
　chopped
400g can chopped tomatoes
200ml/8fl oz red wine
300ml/½ pint vegetable stock
85g/3oz bulghar wheat

❄ **Instant dinner**
Make double, cool half and freeze without the yogurt and cheese. Defrost and simmer until hot and bubbling then serve with the yogurt and grated cheddar.

1　In a large pan, heat the olive oil, then cook the onion and garlic for 5–7 mins until the onion is softened. Add the cumin seeds and paprika, then cook for a further 2 mins. Stir in the sweet potato, red pepper and butternut squash, and toss with the onion and spices for 2 mins.

2　Pour in the tomatoes, red wine and vegetable stock, season, then simmer gently for 15 mins. Stir in the bulghar wheat, cover with a lid, then simmer for 15 mins more until the vegetables are tender, the bulghar wheat is cooked and the liquid has been absorbed. Serve in bowls topped with a spoonful of Greek-style yogurt and some grated cheddar.

Per serving: 299 kcalories, protein 7.3g, carbohydrate 50.4g, fat 7.2g, saturated fat 0.9g, fibre 5.9g, sugar 18.1g, salt 0.38g

Hot beef stew with beans and peppers ❄

When served with rice or cornbread this hearty stew will stretch to serve eight people, so you could make the recipe as below for four and freeze half for another day.

1 Heat 1 tbsp of oil in a large pan with a lid. Season the meat, then cook about one-third over a high heat for 10 mins until browned. Tip on to a plate and repeat with 2 tbsp of oil and the rest of the meat.

2 Add a splash of water and scrape the pan to remove the bits from the base. Add 1 tbsp oil. Turn the heat down, fry the onion and garlic until softened. Return the meat to the pan, add the flour and stir for 1 min. Add the treacle, cumin, tomatoes and stock. Bring to the boil, reduce the heat, cover and simmer for 1¾ hours. Stir occasionally and check that the meat is covered with liquid.

3 Add the peppers and beans, and cook for a further 15 mins. The stew can now be cooled and kept in the fridge for 2 days. Serve in bowls, with soured cream, coriander and cornbread or rice.

Per serving: 400 kcalories, protein 43g, carbohydrate 18g, fat 18g, saturated fat 5g, fibre 4g, sugar 8g, salt 1.2g

Serves 6 ■ prep 15 mins ■ cook 2¾ hours

4 tbsp vegetable oil
1kg/2lb 4oz stewing beef, cut into chunks
1 onion, chopped
2 garlic cloves, chopped
1 tbsp plain flour
1 tbsp black treacle
1 tsp ground cumin
400g can chopped tomatoes
600ml/1 pint beef stock
2 red peppers, deseeded and chopped
410g can cannellini beans, drained and rinsed

❄ **Instant dinner**
Make double and cool half, then freeze in a freezer-proof container before adding the soured cream and coriander. For best results, defrost and transfer to a pan and bring to the boil. Simmer for 20 mins or until the meat is piping hot, then serve.

Chicken casserole with red wine, ham and peppers ❋

Packed with flavour, and cooked in one pot — so this is not only tasty but saves time on the washing up too!

Serves 4 ■ prep 10 mins ■ cook 1¼ hours

2 tbsp olive oil
8 chicken thighs, skin on
1 red pepper, deseeded and quartered
1 green pepper, deseeded and quartered
2 garlic cloves, finely chopped
1 leek, trimmed and thickly sliced
200g/8oz cooked ham, cut into chunks
1 tsp paprika
300ml/½ pint red wine
400g can chopped tomatoes
1 tbsp tomato purée
2 fresh thyme sprigs or ½ tsp dried
2 tbsp fresh parsley leaves, chopped, to serve (optional)

1 Heat oven to 160C/fan 140C/gas 3. Heat the oil in a large flameproof casserole dish and fry the chicken over a high heat until browned all over. Remove with a slotted spoon and set aside. Reduce the heat slightly and add the peppers. Cook for 2 mins, turning, until browned. Add the garlic and leek, cook for 2 mins, then stir in the ham.

2 Sprinkle over the paprika, cook for a couple of seconds, add the wine and bubble for a few mins. Return the chicken to the pan. Tip in the tomatoes, purée and thyme, and mix well. Pour in water just to cover the chicken, and season. Bring to a simmer, cover and transfer to the oven. Cook for 1 hour, until the sauce thickens and chicken is tender. To serve, sprinkle over the parsley and serve with mash.

Per serving: 896 kcalories, protein 71g, carbohydrate 9g, fat 59g, saturated fat 17g, fibre 3g, added sugar none, salt 2.39g

❋ **Instant dinner**
Make double, cool half and freeze before sprinkling with parsley. Defrost in the fridge overnight. Heat oven to 160C/fan 140C/gas 3. Transfer to a casserole dish and reheat for 45 mins until the chicken is piping hot. Sprinkle with parsley (optional), and serve.

Highland beef with pickled walnuts and pastry puffs ❄

This takes a bit of time to make but is worth it. The flavour of the beef stew improves the longer it's kept. You can freeze it or make it up to 3 days ahead and reheat before serving.

Serves 4 ■ prep 30 mins ■ cook 3 hours

for the pastry puffs
½ x 375g pack ready-rolled puff pastry
1 egg, beaten

for the stew
750g/1lb 3oz stewing beef, cut into 5cm/2in pieces, excess fat removed
1 garlic clove, crushed
1 bay leaf
440ml cans dark stout, such as Guinness
40g/1½ oz butter
1½ tbsp olive oil
50g/2oz smoked streaky bacon, roughly chopped
1½ large Spanish onions, finely chopped
1 tbsp plain flour
175ml/6fl oz port
½ x 390g jar pickled walnuts, halved (reserve 1 tbsp pickling vinegar)
1½ tbsp fresh parsley leaves, chopped, plus extra to serve

1 Heat oven to 200C/fan 180C/gas 6. On a floured surface, roll out the pastry a little and stamp out eight 6cm rounds. Put on to a baking sheet and brush with the egg. Sprinkle with salt and bake for 5–7 mins until puffed and golden. Cool on a wire rack, then store in an airtight container until ready to use.

2 Put the beef, garlic and bay leaf in a large non-metallic bowl and pour in the stout. Cover and leave to marinate in the fridge for at least an hour, preferably overnight.

3 Heat oven to 150C/fan 130C/gas 2. Drain the meat and pat dry on kitchen paper. Reserve the marinade.

4 Heat half the butter and half the oil in a large, lidded flameproof and ovenproof casserole dish. Brown the beef in batches.

5 Wipe the dish with kitchen paper, melt the remaining butter and oil, and fry the bacon and onion for 10–15 mins until the onion is golden brown, very soft and well reduced.

6 Stir in the flour until blended, add the port, reserved marinade and beef. Bring to the boil, cover and cook in the oven for 2½–3 hours or until the meat is very tender.

7 Turn up the oven temperature to 200C/fan 180C/gas 6 ready to reheat the pastries. Add the pickled walnuts and reserved pickling vinegar to the casserole, and cook on the hob for a further 30 mins. Stir through the parsley. Reheat the pastries in the oven for 3–4 mins. Serve in bowls, topped with the pastry puffs.

Per serving: 900 kcalories, protein 51g, carbohydrate 37g, fat 54g, saturated fat 17g, fibre 2g, added sugar 5g, salt 1.51g

❄ **Instant dinner**
Make double, following the method to the end of step 6, cool half and put in the fridge or freeze. If chilling, put the meat in a sealed container and store in the fridge for up to 3 days. The pastries will keep in the airtight container until ready to use. If freezing, put the meat and pastries into freezer-proof containers. Freeze for up to 1 month. Defrost completely, to reheat. Follow instructions for step 7.

Light chicken curry ❄

A mild and satisfying dish that's so much tastier – and healthier – than a takeaway.

1 Cook the ginger, garlic and onion in a large pan with the oil until softened. Tip in the chicken and cook until lightly browned, about 5 mins, then add the garam masala and cook for 1 min further.

2 Pour over the stock and simmer for 10 mins until the chicken is cooked through. Mix together the fromage frais and ground almonds. Take the pan off the heat and stir in the fromage-frais mixture. Sprinkle over the sliced almonds, garnish with the coriander and serve with boiled rice, chapatis or naan bread.

Per serving: 243 kcalories, protein 37g, carbohydrate 4g, fat 9g, saturated fat 1g, fibre 1g, sugar 3g, salt 0.31g

❄ **Instant dinner**
Make double then cool and freeze half without adding the fromage-frais mixture. To reheat, defrost the chicken, bring to the boil and simmer for 20 mins or until piping hot, then add the fromage-frais and ground-almond mix and finish off as the recipe states.

Serves 4 ■ prep 15 mins ■ cook 20 mins

small knob root ginger, peeled and finely chopped
1 garlic clove, chopped
1 onion, chopped
1 tbsp vegetable oil
4 boneless skinless chicken breasts, cut into bite-size pieces
1 tsp garam masala
100ml/3½fl oz chicken stock
3 tbsp low-fat fromage frais
2 tbsp ground almonds
handful toasted sliced almonds, to serve
coriander sprigs, to garnish

Goulash in a dash ❄

This spicy dish takes just about half an hour to make from start to finish. Serve with rice or baked potatoes.

1 Heat half the oil in a large non-stick pan and fry the beef for 2 mins, stirring once halfway through. You may need to do this in batches. Tip the meat on to a plate. Heat the remaining oil in the pan (no need to clean) and fry the mushrooms for 2–3 mins until they start to colour.

2 Sprinkle the paprika over the mushrooms, fry briefly, then tip in the potatoes, stock and tomato sauce. Give it all a good stir, cover and simmer for 20 mins until the potatoes are tender. Return the beef to the pan along with any juices, and warm through. Stir in the parsley and a swirl of yogurt, and serve.

Per serving: 299 kcalories, protein 23g, carbohydrate 33g, fat 9g, saturated fat 2g, fibre 3g, added sugar 5g, salt 1.59g

❄ **Instant dinner**
Make double, cool half and freeze before adding the yogurt and parsley. Defrost and put in a pan on the hob. Bring to the boil and simmer for 15 mins or until piping hot, then stir in the parsley and swirl in the yogurt.

Serves 4 ■ prep 5 mins ■ cook 30 mins

1 tbsp vegetable oil
300g/10oz stir-fry beef strips or minute steak, cut into strips
100g/4oz chestnut mushrooms, quartered
2 tsp paprika
500g/1lb 2oz potatoes, peeled and chopped into bite-sized chunks
600ml/1 pint hot beef stock
500g jar tomato-based cooking sauce
handful fresh parsley leaves, roughly chopped
natural yogurt, to serve

Meatloaf ❄

A real crowd-pleaser that is smart enough for a special buffet or easily dresses down for a weekend family supper.

Cuts into 8–10 slices
■ **prep 20 mins** ■ **cook 1 hour**

2 slices fresh white bread, crusts
   removed
500g pack minced pork
1 onion, chopped
1 garlic clove, chopped
big handful fresh parsley, chopped
1 tbsp fresh oregano, chopped, or
   1 tsp dried
4 tbsp grated parmesan
1 egg, beaten
8 slices prosciutto

❄ **Instant dinner**
Make double and freeze half before baking (make sure the pork has not been frozen before). Defrost thoroughly before cooking and follow the method for cooking from step 2. You can also cut it into slices once cooked and freeze, then take out the slices as you need them; it must be completely thawed and piping hot before serving.

1 Heat oven to 190C/fan 170C/gas 5. Put the bread in a food processor or blender and blitz to make crumbs, then tip into a bowl with the pork. Tip the onion, garlic and herbs into the food processor and blitz until finely chopped. Add to the bowl with the parmesan and egg. Finely chop 2 slices of the prosciutto and add to the mix with some salt and pepper. Mix well with a fork.

2 Use the rest of the prosciutto to line a 1.5 litre loaf tin. Spoon in the meatloaf mix and press down well. Flip the overhanging prosciutto over the top, then put the loaf tin into a roasting tin. Pour hot water from the kettle into the roasting tin to come halfway up the loaf tin and bake for 1 hour until the meatloaf shrinks from the sides of tin.

3 Cool for 10 mins, then drain off any excess liquid and turn out on to a board. Cut into thick slices and serve warm or cold with salad.

Per serving (8): 180 kcalories, protein 18g, carbohydrate 5g, fat 10g, saturated fat 4g, fibre 1g, sugar 1g, salt 0.63g

Cheesy leek and potato pie ❄

This pie is made like an extra-large pasty, so you don't need a special dish or ring. Use ready-made pastry for speed, but if you want to make your own, it's easy to do.

Serves 6 ■ prep 10 mins ■ cook 1 hour

3 leeks, thickly sliced
small knob butter
pinch dried rosemary or thyme
450g/1lb potatoes (1 very large baking potato is perfect), chopped into thick slices
140g/5oz cheddar, cut into small chunks
500g pack shortcrust pastry
1 egg, beaten

❄ **Instant dinner**
Make sure you have a baking tray that fits into your freezer. Make double, assemble two pies and freeze one uncooked and covered on its baking tray, for up to 2 months. Defrost overnight, then cook as the recipe states.

MAKE YOUR OWN SAVOURY SHORTCRUST PASTRY
Rub 200g/8oz diced cold butter together with 375g/13oz plain flour, a pinch of salt and a grind of pepper, to form the texture of breadcrumbs. Add a beaten egg and mix to make crumbly dough. Wrap the dough in cling film and chill for 30 mins before using.

1   Put the leeks, butter and herbs in a pan, cover and cook over a low heat for about 20 mins until very soft, stirring occasionally. While the leeks are cooking, put the potatoes in a pan of cold water, bring to the boil and simmer for 4–5 mins until just cooked. Drain the potatoes and stir into the cooked leeks. Leave to cool, stir in the cheese and season with plenty of salt and pepper to taste.

2   Heat oven to 200C/fan 180C/gas 6. Cut the pastry in half and roll out one of the pieces to the size of a dinner plate. Transfer this to a baking sheet and roll the remaining pastry and any trimmings to a round about 5cm bigger than the first. Pile the filling into the middle of the pastry round on the baking sheet, leaving a 4cm border. Brush the border with the beaten egg, then drape over the larger piece of pastry. Trim the edges to neaten, then press the sides together with your thumb. Brush the tart all over with egg. Bake for 35–40 mins until golden. Leave to rest for 10 mins before cutting into wedges.

Per serving: 555 kcalories, protein 14g, carbohydrate 52g, fat 34g, saturated fat 17g, fibre 4g, sugar 2g, salt 0.83g

Fish pie ❄

A classic fish pie is comfort food at its best and a great winter supper dish for family and friends.

1 Put the fish in a frying pan and pour over 500ml of the milk. Stud each onion quarter with a clove, then add to the milk, with the bay leaves. Bring the milk just to the boil (you will see a few small bubbles). Reduce the heat and simmer for 8 mins. Lift the fish on to a plate and strain the milk into a jug to cool. Flake the fish into large pieces in a baking dish.

2 Bring a small pan of water to a gentle boil, then carefully lower the eggs in with a slotted spoon. Bring the water back to a gentle boil (with just a couple of bubbles rising to the surface). Set the timer for 8 mins, cook, then drain and cool in a bowl of cold water. Peel, slice into quarters and arrange on top of the fish, then scatter over the parsley.

3 Melt half the butter in a pan, stir in the flour and cook for 1 min over a medium heat. Take off the heat, pour in a little cold poaching milk, then stir until blended. Continue to add the milk gradually, mixing well until you have a smooth sauce. Return to the heat, bring to the boil and cook for 5 mins, stirring continually, until it coats the back of a spoon. Remove from the heat, season with salt, pepper and nutmeg, then pour over the fish.

4 Heat oven to 200C/fan 180C/gas 6. Boil the potatoes for 20 mins. Drain, season and mash with the remaining butter and milk. Use to top the pie, starting at the edge of the dish and working your way in – push the mash right to the edges to seal. Fluff the top with a fork, sprinkle with cheese, then bake for 30 mins.

Per serving: 824 kcalories, protein 60g, carbohydrate 61g, fat 40g, saturated fat 22g, fibre 4g, sugar 10g, salt 3.12g

❄ **Instant dinner**
Make double, assemble two pies, leaving out the eggs in the one to be frozen. Freeze the unbaked fish pie in a freezer-proof and ovenproof container tightly wrapped in foil. Once defrosted, bake at 200C/fan 180C/gas 6 for 40 mins, or until piping hot.

Serves 4 ■ prep 15 mins ■ cook 1½ hours

400g/14oz skinless white fish fillet
400g/14oz skinless smoked haddock fillet
600ml/1 pint full-fat milk
1 small onion, quartered
4 cloves
2 bay leaves
4 eggs
small bunch fresh parsley leaves, chopped
100g/4oz butter
50g/2oz plain flour
pinch fresh nutmeg, grated
1kg/2lb 4oz floury potatoes, peeled and cut into even-size chunks
50g/2oz cheddar, grated

Italian-style beef ❊

Create a quick, satisfying supper with this rich and easy stew.
You can easily double the recipe if you have friends over.

Serves 4 ■ prep 10 mins
■ cook 20 mins

1 onion, chopped
1 garlic clove, chopped
2 tbsp olive oil
300g pack beef stir-fry strips (or
   use beef steak, thinly sliced)
1 yellow pepper, deseeded and
   chopped
400g can chopped tomatoes
fresh rosemary sprig, chopped
handful pitted olives

1   In a large pan, cook the onion and garlic in olive oil for 5 mins until softened and turning golden. Tip in the beef strips, pepper, tomatoes and rosemary, then bring to the boil.

2   Simmer for 15 mins until the meat is cooked through, adding some boiling water if needed. Stir through the olives and serve with mash or polenta.

Per serving: 225 kcalories, protein 25g, carbohydrate 7g, fat 11g, saturated fat 3g, fibre 2g, sugar 6g, salt 0.87g

❊   **Instant dinner**
Make double, cool half and freeze. To reheat, tip into a large pan, add a splash of water and slowly bring to the boil. Simmer for 20 mins until the meat is piping hot and the sauce is bubbling.

Warming fish stew ❆

A simple stew ideal for cold evenings and relaxed entertaining.

1   Heat the oil in a pan. Tip in the garlic, cumin and paprika, and cook for 1 min. Add 100ml of water and the tomatoes. Bring to the boil, then turn down the heat.

2   Add the pepper, and simmer for 5 mins. Add the fish and simmer for 5 mins. Sprinkle with the coriander and serve with wedges of lemon and fresh crusty bread.

Per serving: 143 kcalories, protein 22g, carbohydrate 5g, fat 4g, saturated fat 1g, fibre 1g, sugar 4g, salt 0.28g

❆ **Instant dinner**
If the fish has not been previously frozen, make double, cool half and freeze before sprinkling with coriander. To reheat, defrost in the fridge overnight then bring to the boil gently. Simmer until piping hot, then sprinkle over the coriander and serve with the lemon wedges.

TIP Concerned about over-fishing? Pollock and organically farmed cod are sustainable options, look for them in most supermarkets.

Serves 4 ▪ prep 5 mins ▪ cook 15 mins

1 tbsp olive oil
2 garlic cloves, crushed
1 tsp ground cumin
½ tsp paprika
200g can chopped tomatoes
1 red pepper, deseeded and
  chopped
450g/1lb white fish fillets, cut into
  chunks
handful fresh coriander leaves,
  roughly chopped
1 lemon, cut into wedges, to serve

Minty pea and potato soup ❄

A few affordable ingredients can be used to whip up a vibrant, fresh-tasting soup.

Serves 4 ▪ prep 5 mins ▪ cook 25 mins

2 tsp vegetable oil
1 onion, chopped
800g/1lb 12oz potatoes, peeled and cut into small chunks
1 litre/1¾ pints vegetable stock
350g/12oz frozen peas
handful fresh mint leaves, chopped

1 Heat the oil in a large pan, then fry the onion for 5 mins until softened. Add the potatoes and stock, then bring to the boil. Cover and simmer for 10–15 mins until tender, adding the peas 2 mins before the end of the cooking time.

2 Use a slotted spoon to remove a quarter of the vegetables from the pan and set aside.

3 Blend the remaining vegetables and stock in a food processor or with an electric hand blender until smooth, then stir through the reserved veg, chopped mint and some seasoning. Serve with crusty bread.

Per serving: 249 kcalories, protein 11g, carbohydrate 48g, fat 3g, saturated fat 1g, fibre 9g, sugar 7g, salt 0.36g

❄ **Instant dinner**
Make double, cool half and freeze before adding the mint. Defrost before reheating, or gently thaw in the pan until hot, then add the chopped mint and adjust the seasoning.

TIP Another great freezer stand-by works well with the flavours of pea soup. Grill a couple of fish fingers, cut into chunks and serve as croutons on the top.

Tomato soup ❄

This soup is the stuff of childhood, and when it's homemade it tastes even better.

Serves 4 for lunch or 6 as a starter ■ **prep 25 mins** ■ **cook 45 mins**

1–1.25kg/2lb 4oz–2lb 12oz ripe
   tomatoes
2 tbsp olive oil
1 medium onion, chopped
1 small carrot, chopped
1 celery stick, chopped
2 squirts of tomato purée (about
   2 tsp)
pinch of sugar
2 bay leaves
1.2 litres/2 pints hot vegetable
   stock (made with boiling water
   and 4 rounded tsp bouillon
   powder or 2 stock cubes)

❄ **Instant dinner**
Make double, following the method to the end of step 5. Cool half and freeze for up to 3 months. Defrost before reheating, if you've time, or reheat gently in a pan then continue with the recipe at step 6.

1 Cut each tomato into quarters and slice off the hard cores (they don't soften during cooking and you'd get hard bits in the soup at the end).

2 Heat the oil in a large heavy-based pan over a low heat. Tip in the onion, carrot and celery, and mix together with a wooden spoon. Cook on a low heat until soft and faintly coloured. This should take about 10 mins, stirring a few times so the veg cooks evenly and doesn't stick to the bottom of the pan.

3 Squeeze in the tomato purée, then stir it around so it coats the vegetables. Add the tomatoes, sprinkle with a good pinch of sugar and a little freshly ground black pepper, then add the bay leaves. Stir to mix everything together, put the lid on the pan and let the tomatoes stew over a low heat for 10 mins until they shrink down and their juices flow nicely. From time to time, give the pan a good shake – this will keep everything well mixed.

4 Slowly pour in the stock and stir well. Turn up the heat and bring to the boil, then turn the heat down to low again and put the lid back on the pan. Cook gently for 25 mins, stirring a couple of times. At the end of cooking the tomatoes will have broken down completely.

5 Remove the pan from the heat, then fish out the bay leaves and discard. Ladle the soup into a blender and blitz until the soup is smooth (you may have to do this in batches, stop the machine and lift the lid to check after about 30 secs), then pour the puréed soup into a large bowl.

6 Pour the puréed soup back into the pan over a medium heat for a few mins, stirring occasionally until you can see bubbles breaking gently on the surface. Check the seasoning then ladle into bowls and serve, or sieve and serve chilled with some cream swirled through.

Per serving (4): 123 kcalories, protein 4g, carbohydrate 13g, fat 7g, saturated fat 1g, fibre 4g, added sugar 1g, salt 1.08g

Chunky cheddar and celeriac soup ❄

Soup is a meal in a bowl, making it a handy supper to have in the freezer.

1 Melt the butter in a large pan. Add the onions and cook for 5 mins until softened, but not coloured. Add the potato, celeriac, stock, sage and lemon zest. Bring to the boil and simmer gently for about 30 mins, until the celeriac is tender and the potato is collapsing. Remove and discard the lemon zest and sage leaves. Stir, breaking-up the potato to thicken the soup a little (at this point you can cool and keep the soup covered in the fridge for up to 2 days).

2 When you're ready to eat, reheat the soup to just simmering. Stir in the cheese until melted. Serve with crispy sage leaves for a special touch.

Per serving: 411 kcalories, protein 21g, carbohydrate 35g, fat 22g, saturated fat 13g, fibre 12g, added sugar none, salt 2.40g

❄ **Instant dinner**
Make double, following the method to the end of step 1. Cool half and freeze for up to 3 months. Defrost slowly in a pan and heat until gently bubbling but not boiling. Finish off as the recipe states in step 2.

Serves 4 ■ prep 15 mins ■ cook 40 mins

1 tbsp butter
3 onions, finely chopped
500g/1lb 2oz floury potatoes, peeled and chopped
2 celeriac (1kg/2lb 4oz in total), peeled and chopped
1 litre/1¾ pints chicken or vegetable stock
4 fresh sage leaves, plus extra to serve (optional, see tip)
2 strips lemon zest
200g/8oz mature cheddar, diced

TIP These crisp sage leaves are an easy way to make this soup look special. Cover the surface of a small pan with vegetable oil. Heat until the surface shimmers, then drop in the sage. Cook for 20–30 seconds, until starting to brown, then lift out and drain on kitchen paper. As the leaves cool they crisp up – if they don't, return them to the hot oil for a few more seconds.

Smoked haddock chowder ❄

A rich, smoky, satisfying dish that is easily doubled.

1   Put the fish in a frying pan with the bay leaf and milk. Bring to a simmer, then cover and set aside for 10 mins. Lift out the fish with a slotted spoon, flake roughly, discarding any bones, and strain the milk.

2   Melt the butter in a large frying pan and cook the onion over a low heat for 3–4 mins until softened. Sprinkle in the flour and stir for 1 min, then tip in the garlic and red pepper, and cook for a further 5 mins. Now stir in the sherry and simmer until almost all the liquid has disappeared.

3   Add the paprika and potatoes, pour in the poaching milk and bring to the boil. Cover and simmer for 15 mins, add the sweetcorn and cook for 5 mins more. Remove from the heat and gently fold in the fish. Scatter over the parsley and serve with garlic bread.

Per serving: 386 kcalories, protein 32g, carbohydrate 35g, fat 10g, saturated fat 6g, fibre 2g, added sugar none, salt 2.63g

❄   **Instant dinner**
Make double, cool half and freeze. Defrost in the fridge overnight. Reheat gently in a pan on the hob until piping hot then add the parsley. Garlic bread is a great freezer stand-by too.

Serves 4 ■ prep 15 mins ■ cook 25 mins

450g/1lb smoked haddock fillet, skinned
1 bay leaf
850ml/1½ pints milk
25g/1oz butter
1 onion, finely chopped
1 tbsp plain flour
1 garlic clove, crushed
1 red pepper, deseeded and roughly chopped
125ml/4fl oz dry sherry
pinch of paprika
200g/8oz floury potatoes, peeled and diced
100g/4oz frozen or canned sweetcorn kernels
handful fresh parsley leaves, chopped, to serve

chapter 2

Weekday suppers and leftover ideas

Who's got the time or inclination to spend hours in the kitchen at the end of a hectic day? These recipes are quick and easy to prepare and also share a couple of common ingredients to help you use up leftovers. By planning two meals at once, you will get the most out of what you buy and dramatically cut your food bills and reduce wastage.

A smart cook will keep some of last night's roast, cook a little extra rice or pasta and keep the remains of the pack of bacon that was bought at the weekend, as they will give you the basics for a new dish at no extra cost.

We've paired up two types of recipe that share ingredients and have called them 'weekday suppers' and 'leftover ideas'. Weekday suppers are coloured orange; they are all easy-to-make ideas, and the majority take less than 30 minutes — perfect for busy weeknights. Next to each weekday supper is a blue leftover idea. These recipes use either surplus raw ingredients or extra cooked quantities of the weekday meal.

For leftover ideas that use cooked quantities from weekday suppers, we've included (in brackets) the extra you need to cook while making the weekday supper to ensure enough leftovers for the second dish. Otherwise, we've chosen raw ingredients that can be bought in large packs for more cost-effective shopping, which create two different meals. All the recipes serve four adults, so, depending on the size of your family, you can choose whether you need to cook the extra to make the leftover idea.

Leftover know-how

■ Use your leftovers wisely — cool them as fast as you can and wrap them well before storing them in the fridge.

■ Casseroles, curries, stews and whole joints of meat will be fine for 2–3 days.

■ Most other leftovers are only good for 24 hours, so if you're not going to use them for supper the next night, why not turn them into a packed lunch instead?

■ You can save a surprising amount of money every year just by packing your own sandwiches. Make them the night before if you don't get time in the morning.

■ If you don't think you'll use up leftovers, avoid pre-packaged products and go to butchers, fishmongers and greengrocers, or the counters in supermarkets where you can weigh out items exactly. Freeze anything you won't use immediately on the day of purchase.

One-pot mushroom and potato curry

Whip up a mid-week veggie treat in just 30 minutes.

1 Heat the oil in a large pan, add the onion and potato. Cover, then cook over a low heat for 5 mins until the potatoes start to soften. Throw in the aubergine and mushrooms, then cook for a few more mins.

2 Stir in the curry paste, pour over the stock and coconut milk. Bring to the boil, then simmer for 10 mins or until the potato is tender. Stir through the coriander and serve with rice. Cook 300g/10oz of basmati rice to serve with the curry — double this if you want to cook enough rice to make the leftover idea too. Cool and chill the leftover rice quickly.

Per serving: 212 kcalories, protein 5g, carbohydrate 15g, fat 15g, saturated fat 9g, fibre 3g, sugar 5g, salt 0.71g

Serves 4 ■ prep 10 mins ■ cook 20 mins

1 tbsp sunflower oil
1 onion, roughly chopped
1 large potato, chopped
1 aubergine, trimmed and chopped
250g/9oz button mushrooms (buy 600g to make the leftover idea)
2–4 tbsp curry paste (depending on how hot you like it)
150ml/¼ pint vegetable stock
400ml can reduced-fat coconut milk
handful fresh coriander leaves, chopped, to garnish

Fast-fix fried rice

Put your own twist on this takeaway favourite that uses leftover rice and mushrooms.

1 Heat the oil in a frying pan, then tip in the beaten eggs. Leave to set for 30 secs–1 min, swirling every now and again until cooked, then tip out and finely slice. Add the bacon and mushrooms to the pan, then fry until golden, about 3 mins. Add the peas, garlic and ginger, then cook for 1 min.

2 Mix together the soy sauce and sugar. Turn up the heat, add the cooked rice to the pan, heat through, then splash in the soy sauce mix. Stir through the egg and serve straight away, with more soy sauce, if you like.

Per serving: 355 kcalories, protein 18g, carbohydrate 48g, fat 11g, saturated fat 3g, fibre 6g, sugar 6g, salt 1.81g

KNOW-HOW For food safety, make sure that leftover rice isn't any more than a day old, that it was chilled quickly and that it has stayed chilled since it was cooked and cooled. Make sure it's piping hot when you use it to make anything else.

Serves 4 ■ prep 5 mins ■ cook 7 mins

4 tsp sunflower oil
2 eggs, beaten
4 rashers bacon, chopped
leftover button mushrooms, sliced (about 350g/12oz)
400g/1lb frozen peas
2 garlic cloves, crushed
small knob root ginger, grated
4 tsp dark soy sauce, plus extra to serve
2 tsp sugar
leftover cooked basmati rice, chilled (about 500g/1lb 2oz)

Pork fillet with roasted vegetables

A great thing about this recipe is that everything roasts in one pan.

**Serves 4 ▪ prep 15 mins
▪ cook 55–60 mins**

4 medium parsnips (about
    550g/1lb 4oz), peeled, cored
    and quartered lengthways
1 butternut squash (about
    650g/1lb 7oz), peeled, deseeded
    and chopped into chunks
    (add 550g/1lb 4oz parsnips
    and squash to make the
    leftover idea)
2 red onions, each cut into 8 wedges
1 tbsp olive oil
zest 1 lemon
2 tsp dried mixed Italian herbs
500g/1lb 2oz lean pork tenderloin,
    in 1 or 2 pieces
1 medium Bramley apple
400ml/14fl oz chicken stock

1   Heat oven to 200C/fan 180C/gas 6. Put all the vegetables including the onions into a roasting tin. Drizzle with the olive oil, season with salt and pepper, then toss everything together.

2   On a plate, mix the lemon zest and the herbs. Roll the pork tenderloin in the mixture, then put it on top of the vegetables. Roast for 40 mins. If making the leftover idea, reserve about 550g/1lb 4oz of the cooked vegetables now.

3   Peel and core the apple and cut into chunks. Scatter the pieces into the roasting tin, then pour in the hot stock and cook for a further 15–20 mins. Slice the pork, arrange on a platter with the veg, then spoon the pan juices over the top.

Per serving: 397 kcalories, protein 34g, carbohydrate 45g, fat 10g, saturated fat 2g, fibre 12g, added sugar none, salt 0.85g

Spiced veg soup

This soup is also tasty if made with Brussels sprouts or carrots.

**Serves 4 ▪ prep 10–15 mins
▪ cook 20–25 mins**

1 tbsp sunflower oil
1 medium onion, chopped
2 celery sticks, chopped
2 medium potatoes (about
    350g/12oz total weight), peeled
    and chopped into small chunks
1 tbsp curry paste
1.2 litres/2 pints vegetable stock
leftover roasted vegetables, such
    as parsnips and squash, roughly
    chopped (about 550g/1lb 4oz)

1   Heat the oil in a large pan and fry the onion for 5 mins until golden. Stir in the celery and fry for 5 mins, then tip in the potatoes and fry for a further 1–2 mins, stirring often.

2   Stir in the curry paste, let it cook for 1–2 mins, then pour in the stock. Bring to the boil and stir. Lower the heat, cover and simmer for 15–20 mins until the potatoes are tender.

3   Tip the leftover veg into the pan and warm through. Pour into a blender and whizz to a smooth purée. Thin down with hot water or stock, if you like (we added 300ml), then taste for seasoning. Serve in bowls with spoonfuls of crème fraîche swirled on top.

Per serving: 233 kcalories, protein 6g, carbohydrate 30.4g, fat 10.4g, saturated fat 1.1g, fibre 8g, sugar 10.8g, salt 0.94g

TIP You can vary the flavour of homemade soups by using different curry pastes as the base. You can make it as hot or as mild as you like so play around with the amounts.

Oven-baked pepper risotto ❄

Take the (tiny) effort of stirring out of risotto-making with this easy baked version.

1   Heat oven to 200C/fan 180C/gas 6. Heat the oil in an ovenproof pan, then fry the onion for a few mins until softened. Turn up the heat, tip in the rice, stir, then fry for 1 min more. Pour in the wine, if using, and stir until absorbed. Pour in the tomatoes, peppers and 400ml of the stock. Cover and bake in the oven for 25 mins until the rice is tender and creamy.

2   Stir in the remaining stock and the parsley, season. Reserve a third of the risotto now for the leftover idea. Refrigerate it as soon as it has cooled. Serve the rest sprinkled with parmesan.

Per serving: 252 kcalories, protein 6.9g, carbohydrate 53.3g, fat 2.7g, saturated fat 0.3g, fibre 3.8g, sugar 6.7g, salt 1.09g

Serves 4 ▪ prep 5 mins ▪ cook 30 mins

1 tbsp sunflower oil
1 onion, chopped
350g/12oz risotto rice
125ml/4fl oz white wine
   (or use more stock)
400g can chopped tomatoes
250g/9oz frozen roasted peppers
600ml/1 pint vegetable stock
handful fresh parsley leaves,
   chopped
grated parmesan, to serve
(reserve ⅓ cooked quantity to make the leftover idea)

Risotto cakes

These are a good way to use up leftover risotto, and they taste great served with crispy bacon, if you have some.

1   Shape handfuls of the leftover risotto into burger shapes. Dip into seasoned flour, then beaten egg, and finally into the breadcrumbs to coat.

2   Heat the oil in a non-stick frying pan and fry the burgers for 4 mins each side, then serve with crisp bacon rashers and salad.

Per serving: 331 kcalories, protein 10.7g, carbohydrate 50.9g, fat 10.8g, saturated fat 1.7g, fibre 2.6g, sugar 4.1g, salt 1.14g

Serves 4 ▪ prep 5 mins ▪ cook 10 mins

leftover risotto, chilled overnight
   (about 450g/1lb)
flour, seasoned with salt and
   pepper
2 eggs, beaten
4 handfuls breadcrumbs
2 tbsp sunflower oil

Chunky minestrone ❄

Here one cabbage makes two different meals.

Serves 4 ▪ **prep 10–15 mins** ▪ **cook 30 mins**

3 large carrots, roughly chopped
1 large onion, roughly chopped
4 celery sticks, roughly chopped
1 tbsp olive oil
2 garlic cloves, crushed
2 large potatoes, chopped into small chunks
2 tbsp tomato purée
2 litres/3½ pints vegetable stock
400g can chopped tomatoes
410g can cannellini or butter beans
140g/5oz spaghetti
½ Savoy cabbage head, shredded (use the other half to make the leftover idea)

1 In a food processor, whizz the carrots, onion and celery into small pieces. Heat the oil in a pan, add the processed vegetables, garlic and potatoes, then cook over a high heat for 5 mins until softened.

2 Stir in the tomato purée, stock and tomatoes. Bring to the boil, then turn down the heat and simmer, covered, for 10 mins.

3 Snap the spaghetti strands in half, then tip them and the beans into the pan. Cook for a further 10 mins, adding the cabbage for the final 2 mins. Season to taste and serve with crusty bread.

Per serving: 420 kcalories, protein 18g, carbohydrate 79g, fat 6g, saturated fat 1g, fibre 16g, sugar 24g, salt 1.11g

Spicy bubble and squeak cake ❄

Every thrifty cook should have this twist on a classic up their sleeve.

1 Tip the parsnips into a pan of cold water with the turmeric and a little salt. Boil for about 12 mins until they are very tender.

2 While the parsnips are cooking, blanch the cabbage in another pan of boiling water for 3 mins until tender, adding the peas for the final min, then drain well.

3 Drain the parsnips, then tip back into the pan and roughly mash with the lemon juice and half the butter. Beat in all the other ingredients, except the remaining butter, then season with salt.

4 Heat the remaining butter in a non-stick frying pan. Press the veg mixture into the pan. Cook until crisp underneath, then turn over with a fish slice. Cook until crisp on the other side, slide on to a plate and flip back into the pan again. Keep on doing this until the cake is crisp all over. Serve cut into wedges and sprinkled with the coriander, if you like.

Per serving (4): 277 kcalories, protein 7g, carbohydrate 33g, fat 14g, saturated fat 7g, fibre 12g, sugar 15g, salt 0.27g

Serves 4 as a veggie main or 8 as a side dish ▪ **prep 15 mins** ▪ **cook 30 mins**

800g/1lb 12oz parsnips, peeled, cored and chopped into chunks
1 tsp turmeric
leftover Savoy cabbage, finely shredded (about ½ head)
large handful frozen peas
juice ½ lemon
50g/2oz butter
1 tsp cumin seeds
1 tbsp garam masala
handful fresh coriander leaves, chopped
1 red chilli, deseeded and chopped
2 fresh coriander sprigs, to garnish (optional)

Smoked salmon and pea frittata

Make the most of salmon trimmings, which are a clever budget buy, often costing far less than normal smoked salmon.

Serves 4 ▪ prep 20–25 mins ▪ cook 20–25 mins

500g/1lb 2oz new potatoes, thinly chopped
8 eggs
200g/8oz smoked salmon trimmings
(buy 250g pack to make the leftover idea)
2 tbsp fresh dill, chopped
100g/4oz frozen petit pois or peas
3 tbsp olive oil

TIP Fresh herbs freeze well. Simply chop and divide among the holes of an ice-cube tray. Top up with water and freeze. Once frozen, you can pop them in a freezer bag to free up the ice-cube tray.

1 Cook the potatoes in a pan of boiling salted water until just tender, about 10 mins. Drain well and leave to cool slightly.

2 Crack the eggs into a bowl, beat with a fork until lightly foamy, then stir in the smoked salmon trimmings, dill, peas and plenty of salt and pepper. Then, stir in the potatoes.

3 Heat the olive oil in a large non-stick frying pan, carefully pour in the egg mixture and cook over a fairly low heat for 10–15 mins, until the egg is starting to set just under the surface.

4 Put a plate that is slightly larger than the pan over the top and invert the frittata on to it. Slide it back into the pan and cook for a further 5 mins to brown the underside. Slide on to a plate and leave to cool for 5 mins before cutting into wedges.

Per serving: 356 kcalories, protein 31.3g, carbohydrate 22.5g, fat 16.3g, saturated fat 4.3g, fibre 2.6g, sugar 2.3g, salt 2.85g

Smoked salmon and bean dip with crispy pittas

A clever idea for leftover smoked salmon and dill. The pittas become crunchy in the oven, making them unbelievably moreish.

1   Tip the beans into a food processor with the yogurt and blend until smooth. Add the salmon and pulse, keeping the salmon quite chunky. Tip into a bowl and stir in the dill, lemon juice, and season. This can be made up to a day ahead.

2   Heat oven to 200C/fan 180C/gas 6. Tear the pittas and arrange in two roasting tins. Drizzle with the oil and sprinkle with the sea salt and dill. Bake for 7 mins until crisp. Put the bowl of dip on a platter and surround with the pitta crisps.

Per serving: 220 kcalories, protein 11.4g, carbohydrate 30.9g, fat 6.5g, saturated fat 2.1g, fibre 2.8g, sugar 2.6g, salt 1.84g

**Serves 4 ■ prep 10 mins
■ cook 10 mins**

for the dip
200g/8oz canned cannellini beans, drained and rinsed
100g tub Greek yogurt
leftover smoked salmon trimmings (about 50g/2oz)
½ tbsp fresh dill, chopped
½ tbsp lemon juice
for the pittas
3 pitta breads
1 tbsp olive oil
sea salt flakes and 1 tbsp fresh dill, chopped, to sprinkle

Good-for-you bolognese ❄

A great one for kids, this is packed with veg, but they'll never guess.

Serves 4 ■ prep 15 mins
■ cook 30 mins

2 tsp olive oil
2 onions, chopped
6 carrots, chopped
3 courgettes, chopped
140g/5oz button mushrooms
2 garlic cloves, crushed
2 x 400g cans chopped tomatoes
1½ tbsp Worcestershire sauce
300ml/½ pint boiling water
800g/1lb 12oz lean minced beef
large handful fresh basil leaves
1½ tbsp gravy granules
(reserve 500g/1lb 2oz cooked
quantity to make the leftover idea)
400g/14oz spaghetti, to serve

1   Heat the oil in a large frying pan and add the onion. Cook gently for a few mins, then add the carrots, courgettes and mushrooms, and fry for 5 more mins. Stir in the garlic after 4 mins.

2   Tip in the tomatoes, Worcestershire sauce and the boiling water, then season to taste. Bring to the boil, cover, then simmer for 15 mins until tender. Meanwhile, heat a non-stick pan and add the mince. Break it up with a wooden spatula and cook for 10 mins, stirring until browned all over.

3   Add the basil leaves (reserve a few) to the veg sauce, then put a stick blender into the pan and blend until smooth. Pour the sauce and gravy granules into the mince, then stir to thicken. Cover and simmer for 15 mins. If making the leftover idea, reserve 500g now.

4   Meanwhile, boil the pasta according to the pack instructions. When cooked, drain, reserving a small cup of cooking water. Mix the spaghetti with the sauce and reserved water, then serve, topped with a few more basil leaves.

Per serving: 673 kcalories, protein 50.9g, carbohydrate 94.2g, fat 12.8g, saturated fat 4g, fibre 8.9g, sugar 19.4g, salt 1.41g

Shepherd's pie jackets

Cook the potatoes in the microwave for a really speedy supper.

Serves 4 ■ prep 10–15 mins
■ cook 25 mins

4 baking potatoes
leftover bolognese
   (about 500g/1lb 2oz)
splash of milk
knob of butter
50g/2oz mature cheddar, grated

1   Put the potatoes in the microwave on High for 20 mins until cooked through. While they're cooking, tip the leftover mince mix into a pan and simmer until hot and bubbling.

2   Cut each potato in half and scoop the flesh into a bowl, leaving a thin layer inside the potato skin. Break up the flesh with a fork, then season and mash in the milk and butter until smooth and creamy.

3   Heat the grill to high. Put the potatoes skin-side down in a shallow roasting tin and spoon in the mince mix. Top them with the mash and sprinkle with the cheese. Grill until the cheese has melted and the filling is hot. Serve with steamed green vegetables.

Per serving: 329 kcalories, protein 17.3g, carbohydrate 43.5g, fat 10.7g, saturated fat 5.4g, fibre 4.3g, sugar 5.2g, salt 0.63g

Cauliflower cheese

The quick cheese sauce in this recipe is so handy you'll find lots of uses for it. Try it with lasagne, pasta and as a sauce for fish.

1   Heat the grill to high. Fill a large pan with water and bring to the boil. Meanwhile, break the cauliflower into even-size florets. Drop into the pan and boil for about 7 mins, or until very tender.

2   Mix the crème fraîche with the grated cheese in a small pan and warm until heated through, but not boiling. Put the Swiss cheese, hazelnuts and breadcrumbs in a bowl and mix together.

3   Drain the cauliflower and put in the bottom of a large, shallow baking dish. Pour the warmed sauce over the cauliflower, covering it evenly, then sprinkle with the breadcrumbs. Put under the grill for 5 mins, or until the cheese is bubbling and the breadcrumbs are golden and crusty.

Per serving: 463 kcalories, protein 21g, carbohydrate 15.4g, fat 35.7g, saturated fat 19.6g, fibre 4.2g, sugar 6.5g, salt 0.99g

Serves 4 ■ prep 10 mins ■ cook 20 mins

1 large cauliflower (about 1kg/2lb 4oz)
200ml/8fl oz crème fraîche
100g/4oz mature cheddar, grated
100g/4oz Swiss cheese, such as Gruyère or Emmental, grated
25g/1oz toasted hazelnuts, crushed
50g/2oz breadcrumbs
(reserve 250g/9oz cooked quantity to make the leftover idea)

Cheesy gammon grills

A quick dish that is sure to become a firm family favourite.

1   Heat the grill to high. Snip the sides of the gammon steaks with kitchen scissors so they don't curl up too much when they cook. Put the gammon on to a baking sheet, then grill on one side for about 10 mins until the fat is crisp. Meanwhile, heat the cauliflower cheese in a pan and stir in the wholegrain mustard.

2   When the gammon is crisp, flip it over and cook on the other side for about 10 mins. Spoon the cauliflower mix over the gammon, sprinkle with cheese, then grill for 5 mins until bubbling and golden.

Per serving: 295 kcalories, protein 27.7g, carbohydrate 3.5g, fat 18.9g, saturated fat 8.9g, fibre 1.1g, sugar 1.6g, salt 3.24g

Serves 4 ■ prep 5 mins ■ cook 25 mins

4 small raw gammon steaks
leftover cauliflower cheese (about 250g/9oz)
1 tbsp wholegrain mustard
1 tbsp grated cheddar

Thai satay stir-fry

Pre-prepared stir-fry veg isn't always cheap, but here a large pack makes two meals, so there's no waste.

Serves 4 ▪ prep 5 mins
▪ cook 10 mins

3 tbsp crunchy peanut butter
3 tbsp sweet chilli sauce
2 tbsp soy sauce
300g/10oz straight-to-wok noodles
   (buy a 600g pack and reserve
   ½ to make the leftover idea)
1 tbsp sunflower oil
thumb-size piece root ginger,
   peeled and grated
300g/10oz stir-fry vegetables with
   peppers and mangetout
   (buy 650g pack and reserve half
   to make the leftover idea)
handful fresh basil leaves
25g/1oz roasted peanuts, roughly
   chopped (buy enough peanuts
   to make the leftover idea)

1   Mix the peanut butter, chilli sauce, 100ml of cold water and the soy sauce to make a smooth satay sauce. Put the noodles in a bowl and pour boiling water over them. Stir gently to separate, then drain thoroughly.

2   Heat the oil in a wok, then stir-fry the ginger and harder pieces of veg from the stir-fry mix (such as peppers) for 2 mins. Add the noodles and the rest of the veg, then stir-fry over a high heat for 1-2 mins until the veg are just cooked.

3   Push the veg to one side of the pan, then pour the peanut sauce into the other side, tilting the pan. Bring to the boil, then mix the sauce with the stir-fry. Sprinkle over the basil leaves and peanuts to serve.

Per serving: 304 kcalories, protein 9.6g, carbohydrate 38.4g, fat 13.5g, saturated fat 2.3g, fibre 4.7g, sugar 10.5g, salt 1.97g

Speedy noodle soup

A quick-and-easy comforting supper.

Serves 4 ▪ prep 2 mins
▪ cook 5 mins

1 litre/1¾ pints vegetable stock
2–3 squeezes chilli paste
4 tsp soy sauce
leftover straight-to-wok noodles
   (about 300g/10oz)
leftover stir-fry veg
   (about 350g/12oz)
leftover roasted peanuts, crushed
   to serve (about 50g/2oz)

1   Bring the stock to the boil in a pan, stir in the chilli paste and soy sauce, then drop in the straight-to-wok noodles. Simmer for a few mins until all the noodles have separated.

2   Add the stir-fry veg, reserving any leafy bits until later. Simmer for 1 min until the veg is just tender. Stir in the leafy veg, then simmer for 1 min more. Serve in deep bowls, scattered with crushed peanuts.

Per serving: 163 kcalories, protein 6.2g, carbohydrate 32.8g, fat 1.7g, saturated fat 0.2g, fibre 5g, sugar 5.7g, salt 1.28g

20-minute rice supper

Make the most of the microwave to speed up the cooking time.

Serves 4 ■ prep 5 mins ■ cook 15 mins

300g/10oz long grain rice
600ml/1 pint vegetable or fish stock
1 tbsp korma paste
2 large smoked mackerel fillets, skinned (buy 4 mackerel fillets to make the leftover idea)
100g/4oz frozen peas
3 tbsp low-fat crème fraîche
2 hard-boiled eggs, quartered
handful fresh coriander leaves, to garnish

1 Tip the rice into a large microwave-proof container. Mix together the stock and korma paste, then pour over the rice. Cover with cling film and pierce a few times with a fork, then microwave for 6 mins on High.

2 Break the mackerel into large chunks and stir through the rice along with the peas and crème fraîche, then microwave for 6–8 mins more on Medium until the rice is tender. Top with the eggs and serve sprinkled with the coriander.

Per serving: 677 kcalories, protein 27.7g, carbohydrate 69.5g, fat 33.9g, saturated fat 8.8g, fibre 2g, sugar 2.1g, salt 2.13g

KNOW-HOW Much underused, the microwave can be a handy tool in the kitchen, cutting cooking times by up to 60 per cent and using about one-third of the power of a conventional oven. They come into their own when ingredients and meals need defrosting quickly or when everyone eats at different times.

Hot smoked mackerel jackets

There's no need to get into a rut with your baked spud fillings; this easy idea using leftover mackerel fillets takes minutes to prepare.

Serves 4 ■ prep 5 mins ■ cook 15 mins

4 medium baking potatoes
2–3 tbsp horseradish sauce (or to taste)
100ml/4fl oz milk, warmed
3 bunches spring onions, finely chopped
leftover smoked mackerel fillets, skinned and flaked (about 2 small fillets)

1 Cook the potatoes in the microwave on High for 10 mins until softened. Halve the potatoes and scoop out the flesh into a bowl, leaving a shell of potato around the skin. Heat the grill to high.

2 Mash the potato flesh with the horseradish sauce and milk until smooth and creamy, then fold in the spring onions and mackerel. Season to taste. Spoon the mash back into the potato skins. Put on a baking sheet and grill for 5 mins until the mash is heated through and golden on top.

Per serving: 523 kcalories, protein 19.6g, carbohydrate 76.7g, fat 17.4g, saturated fat 4.1g, fibre 5.9g, sugar 5g, salt 1.23g

TIP To bake your potatoes in the oven, heat to 180C/fan 160C/gas 4 and bake for 1 hour until cooked and crisp on the outside.

Spanish spinach omelette

A large omelette makes a great family supper as it keeps well at room temperature, so everyone can cut portions as they come in.

1 Tip the spinach into a large colander and bring a kettleful of water to the boil. Slowly pour the water over the spinach until wilted, then cool under cold water. Squeeze all the liquid out of the spinach and set aside.

2 Heat the grill to high. Heat the oil in a non-stick flameproof frying pan and gently cook the onion and potato for about 10 mins until the potato is soft. While the onion is cooking, beat the eggs in a large bowl and season with salt and pepper. Stir the spinach into the potatoes, then pour in the eggs and cook, stirring occasionally, until nearly set, then flash the omelette under the grill to set the top. Ease the omelette on to a plate, then flip over back into the pan. Finish cooking on the underside and turn out on to a board. Serve cut into eight wedges. Reserve half for the leftover idea now.

Per serving: 209 kcalories, protein 12.1g, carbohydrate 11.4g, fat 13.1g, saturated fat 2.9g, fibre 2g, sugar 2.4g, salt 0.46g

Cuts into 8 slices
■ **prep 10 mins** ■ **cook 20 mins**

400g bag spinach leaves
3 tbsp olive oil
1 large onion, finely chopped
2 large potatoes, peeled and finely chopped
10 eggs
(this serves 8 people so you can reserve half to make the leftover idea)

Omelette sandwiches

After an omelette supper, try an omelette sandwich – a delicacy in Spain – for lunch or a light evening meal the next day.

Spread the ciabatta rolls with mayo and fill with the omelette and sliced tomato.

Per serving: 567 kcalories, protein 22.4g, carbohydrate 59.7g, fat 28.2g, saturated fat 5.5g, fibre 5.1g, sugar 6.4g, salt 2.17g

Serves 4 ■ **prep 5 mins**

4 ciabatta rolls
4 tbsp mayonnaise
leftover Spanish spinach omelette
    (about 4 wedges)
4 tomatoes, chopped

Creamy mushroom spaghetti

Turn a few rashers of bacon, some mushrooms, cheese and spinach into a satisfying midweek supper.

Serves 4 ▪ prep 10 mins ▪ cook 15 mins

400g/14oz dried spaghetti
6 rashers smoked streaky bacon, rind removed and cut into strips (buy a pack of 10–12 rashers to make the leftover idea)
250g pack chestnut or button mushrooms, sliced
200g/8oz baby leaf spinach, washed (buy 300g to make the leftover idea)
100g/4oz blue cheese, crumbled (buy 240g to make the leftover idea)

1 Bring a large pan of water to the boil, then cook the spaghetti according to the pack instructions.

2 Meanwhile, fry the bacon in a large frying pan for 5 mins, until starting to crisp. Tip in the mushrooms, then fry for 3 mins until cooked. Drain the pasta and tip into the frying pan along with the spinach and cheese. Toss everything together over a low heat until the spinach has wilted and the cheese melted.

Per serving: 505 kcalories, protein 24g, carbohydrate 75g, fat 14g, saturated fat 7g, fibre 5g, sugar 4g, salt 1.80g

Warm stilton salad

This autumnal salad is also smart enough for entertaining.

Serves 4 as a light supper ▪ prep 15 mins ▪ cook 20 mins

leftover bacon, rind removed (about 4 rashers)
3 ripe pears, peeled, cored and chopped
leftover blue cheese, chopped into small cubes (about 140g/5oz)
leftover baby spinach, washed (about 100g/4oz)
for the dressing
1 tbsp sherry or red wine vinegar
1 tsp clear honey
1 tsp wholegrain mustard
2 tbsp olive oil

1 Use kitchen scissors or a sharp knife to snip the bacon into fat matchsticks. Heat a small, dry frying pan on a medium heat and add the bacon. Cook for about 5 mins, until the bacon is crisp.

2 To make the dressing, reduce the heat in the pan to low and stir in 1 tbsp water, then the vinegar, honey and mustard. Stir, scraping up any residue stuck to the pan. Stir in the oil and season to taste.

3 Meanwhile, heat a griddle pan or grill and cook the pears for about 5 mins on each side, until browned. Place in a bowl and mix with the cubes of cheese (this melts the cheese a little, making it nice and squidgy). Tip the spinach into a serving bowl, and scatter the cheese and pear mixture over. Top with the warm bacon and dressing and serve immediately.

Per serving: 305 kcalories, protein 13g, carbohydrate 13g, fat 23g, saturated fat 11g, fibre 3g, added sugar 1g, salt 1.50g

Kale pasta with chilli and anchovy

Anchovies and robust greens are a classic partnership, but if you want to make it vegetarian, swap the anchovy for crumbled vegetarian goat's cheese and just stir it through at the end.

Serves 4 ■ prep 15 mins
■ cook 20 mins

500g/1lb 2oz dried penne
   (add 300g/10oz pasta to
   make leftover idea)
 4 tbsp olive oil
1 red chilli, deseeded and finely
   chopped
2 garlic cloves, finely chopped
4 anchovies, finely chopped
200g/8oz young kale, shredded
juice ½ lemon
50g/2oz parmesan, ½ finely
   grated, ½ shaved

1   Cook the pasta according to the pack instructions. While it's cooking, heat half the oil in a pan, then sizzle the chilli, garlic and anchovies. Add the kale, then gently fry until tender, adding a drop of water if needed.

2   Drain the pasta, reserving a few tbsp of cooking water. If making the leftover idea, reserve the extra pasta now, drizzling it with oil to prevent it from sticking together. Toss the pasta and water through the kale, adding the rest of the olive oil, lemon juice and grated parmesan. Serve scattered with the parmesan shavings.

Per serving: 613 kcalories, protein 22.4g, carbohydrate 96g, fat 18.2g, saturated fat 4.3g, fibre 5.5g, sugar 3.7g, salt 0.73g

Hot pasta salad

Any leftover pasta will taste much better the next day if dressed in a little oil while still warm.

1 Blanch the leftover pasta in boiling water to reheat or, if making from scratch, cook the pasta according to the pack instructions. Meanwhile, tip the mayonnaise, lemon juice and 1 tbsp of the tuna oil into a large bowl and mix. Drain the rest of the oil from the tuna, then flake the fish into the bowl and mix well.

2 Drain the pasta and toss it with the mayonnaise mixture, peppers and onion. Scatter over the rocket just before serving.

Per serving: 478 kcalories, protein 21.8g, carbohydrate 64.1g, fat 16.7g, saturated fat 2.7g, fibre 4.1g, sugar 7.7g, salt 0.50g

Serves 4 ■ prep 5 mins
■ cook 15 mins

leftover cooked penne
  (about 600g/1lb 5oz)
4 tbsp mayonnaise
juice ½ lemon
200g can tuna in olive oil
2 red peppers, deseeded and
  finely chopped
1 red onion, halved and finely
  chopped
large handful fresh rocket leaves

Oriental bangers and mash ❄

A deliciously sticky sauce transforms the humble sausage.

Serves 4 ■ prep 5 mins
■ cook 20 mins

1kg/2lb 4oz Maris Piper or King Edward potatoes, peeled and chopped into chunks
(add 500g/1lb 2oz potatoes to make the leftover idea)
100ml/4fl oz milk
6 spring onions, finely chopped
12 pork and chilli sausages
2 tbsp vegetable oil
600ml/1 pint beef stock
4 tbsp sweet chilli sauce

1 Boil the potatoes in water for 15–20 mins, or until tender. Drain, then mash with the milk. Set aside the extra mashed potato for the leftover idea. Season to taste, then fold in the spring onions.

2 In a frying pan, cook the sausages in the oil for about 10 mins, turning them every so often to brown evenly. Pour the stock in with the sausages. Bring to the boil, then reduce the heat and simmer for 5 mins until beginning to thicken. Stir in the chilli sauce, heat through, then serve with the mash.

Per serving: 794 kcalories, protein 36g, carbohydrate 65g, fat 45g, saturated fat 13g, fibre 4g, sugar 9g, salt 4.02g

Minted salmon and pea fish cakes ❄

A family favourite, using leftover mashed potatoes. You can make these into mini bites for smaller children.

Serves 4 ■ prep 10 mins ■ cook 10 mins

410g can pink or red salmon, drained
140g/5oz frozen peas, defrosted
handful fresh mint leaves, roughly chopped
1 tbsp tartare sauce
leftover mashed potatoes
  (about 500g/1lb 2oz)
3 tbsp plain flour, for dusting
3 tbsp vegetable oil
lemon halves, to serve

TIP These versatile fish cakes can be made with the same amount of tuna or 200g/ 8oz crumbled feta to make them vegetarian.

1 Flake the salmon into a bowl, removing any skin and large bones. Add the peas, mint, tartare sauce and mashed potato, and season to taste. Mix well, then, using floured hands, shape into eight flat fish cakes. Dust with flour.

2 Heat the oil in a large frying pan over a medium heat. Fry the fish cakes in 2 batches for 3–4 mins each side, turning carefully with a fish slice or spatula, until golden and crisp. Serve with lemon halves to squeeze.

Per serving: 368 kcalories, protein 25g, carbohydrate 34g, fat 15g, saturated fat 2g, fibre 4g, added sugar none, salt 1g

Boiled bacon with cabbage

Boiled bacon is always well received, whatever the occasion, but we especially love the leftover sandwiches the next day!

Serves 6 ■ prep 20 mins ■ cook 2 hours

1.3kg/3lb piece smoked bacon
   (reserve 85g/3oz cooked
   quantity to make leftover idea)
1 onion, peeled and studded with
   6 cloves
large bunch fresh herbs tied
   together, including bay, thyme
   and parsley stalks
1 bunch new-season carrots
   (about 12 in total), scrubbed
   and trimmed
for the mustard sauce
142ml pot double cream
150ml/¼ pint stock, from the bacon
3 tbsp English mustard
handful fresh parsley, chopped

1   Put the bacon in a stockpot with the onion and herbs, then cover with water. Bring to a simmer, then cook for 45 mins, topping up with water if needed. Add the carrots, then continue to cook for 15 mins. Ladle 150ml of the bacon stock into a smaller pan and set aside. Add the cabbage wedges to the stockpot, then continue to cook everything for another 10–15 mins until the cabbage is tender, but not overcooked.

2   Meanwhile, make the sauce. Pour the cream into the 150ml of reserved stock and bring to the boil. Simmer for a few mins, then whisk in the mustard and parsley. Season with salt and pepper to taste.

3   Remove the meat from the stock, then carve into thick slices. If making the leftover idea, reserve the meat now. Serve on a platter with the cabbage and carrots, and moisten with a trickle of stock. Serve the sauce in a jug along with some boiled and buttered new potatoes on the side.

Per serving: 611 kcalories, protein 30.4g, carbohydrate 6.9g, fat 51.5g, saturated fat 21.9g, fibre 2.5g, sugar 6.3g, salt 4.15g

Ham and leek cobbler ❄

Serves 4 ■ prep 10 mins ■ cook 30 mins

450g/1lb leeks, chopped
2½ tbsp olive oil
450ml/16fl oz vegetable stock
100g/4oz self-raising flour, plus
   extra for rolling out
75ml/2½fl oz fat-free natural
   yogurt
1 tsp fresh thyme leaves, plus
   extra, to garnish
140g/5oz frozen peas
leftover cooked bacon,
   shredded (about 85g/3oz)
1 apple, grated

1   Heat oven to 200C/fan 180C/gas 6. Cook the leeks in a large pan with ½ teaspoon of oil, stirring for 5 mins until starting to soften then add the stock and simmer for 5 mins.

2   Meanwhile, tip the flour into a bowl, make a well in the centre and add the yogurt, remaining oil, thyme leaves and a couple of pinches of salt. Using a cutlery knife mix into a soft dough. Take a quarter at a time and shape into rounds on a lightly floured surface.

3   Stir the peas, ham and grated apple into the leeks and divide among four individual pie dishes (or one large dish). Top each with a scone, scatter with a bit more thyme and bake for 20 mins.

Per serving: 264 kcalories, protein 12.5g, carbohydrate 34.6g, fat 9.3g, saturated fat 1.5g, fibre 6.3g, sugar 9.8g, salt 1.02g

Caraway roast carrot and feta salad

A great, fresh-tasting veggie dish.

1 Heat oven to 200C/fan 180C/gas 6 and boil the carrots for 4 mins in a pan of water. Drain well, then tip on to a large baking sheet and toss with the caraway seeds, 1 tbsp of olive oil, the orange zest and some seasoning. Roast for 20 mins until golden and tender.

2 Cut away the pith from the oranges. Hold the orange over a salad bowl then cut free each segment, catching the juice and segments in the bowl. Squeeze any remaining juice out of the membranes, repeat with the other orange, then add the remaining oil, red wine vinegar, seeds and seasoning, and give everything a good stir.

3 Gently combine the dressing with the roasted carrots and spinach. Divide among four plates and scatter over the feta to serve.

Per serving: 260 kcalories, protein 8.8g, carbohydrate 21.3g, fat 16.1g, saturated fat 4.7g, fibre 6.2g, sugar 18.7g, salt 0.96g

Serves 4 ▪ prep 5 mins ▪ cook 25 mins

600g/1lb 5oz carrots, peeled and halved or quartered lengthways
2 tsp caraway seeds
2 tbsp olive oil
zest 2 oranges
1 tbsp red wine vinegar
4 large handfuls spinach leaves
2 tbsp mixed seeds, such as pumpkin, sunflower and linseed
100g/4oz feta, crumbled (buy 240g to make the leftover idea)

Tomato and feta pasta sauce

Leftover feta with tomatoes makes a good coating for pasta.

1 Cook the pasta according to the pack instructions.

2 Meanwhile, tip the chopped tomatoes, the dried oregano, sugar and some freshly ground black pepper into a pan. Simmer for 5 mins, then crumble in the feta.

3 Toss with the cooked, drained pasta, and serve.

Per serving: 541 kcalories, protein 21.7g, carbohydrate 98.6g, fat 9.4g, saturated fat 4.8g, fibre 4.9g, sugar 6g, salt 1.17g

Serves 4 ▪ prep 5 mins ▪ cook 5 mins

500g/1lb 2oz dried pasta
400g can chopped tomatoes with garlic or onion
½ tsp dried oregano
½ tsp sugar
leftover feta (about 140g/5oz)

Chicken biryani

Make this Indian dish for four, and there'll still be enough leftovers for a salad the next day.

Serves 4 ■ prep 10 mins ■ cook 30 mins

300g/10oz basmati rice
25g/1oz butter
1 large onion, finely chopped
1 bay leaf
3 cardamom pods
1 small cinnamon stick
1 tsp ground turmeric
4 skinless chicken breasts, chopped into large chunks
4 tbsp curry paste (we used a balti paste)
85g/3oz raisins
850ml/1½ pints chicken stock
handful fresh coriander leaves, chopped, and toasted flaked almonds, to serve
(reserve ⅓ to make the leftover idea too)

1 Soak the rice in warm water for 10 mins, then wash in cold water until the water runs clear. Heat the butter in a pan and cook the onion with the bay leaf and the other whole spices for 10 mins. Sprinkle in the turmeric, then add chicken and curry paste, and cook until the aromas are released.

2 Stir the rice into the pan along with the raisins, then pour over the stock. Place a tight-fitting lid on the pan and bring to a hard boil, then lower the heat to a minimum and cook the rice for another 5 mins. Turn off the heat and leave for 10 mins. Stir well, mixing through half the coriander. Reserve a third of the risotto now for the leftover idea. Refrigerate as soon as it has cooled. To serve, scatter over the rest of the coriander and the toasted almonds.

Per serving: 283 kcalories, protein 21.9g, carbohydrate 37.1g, fat 6.3g, saturated fat 2g, fibre 1g, sugar 8.7g, salt 1.04g

Coronation chicken rice salad

A supper fit for a queen! It works well with other curry leftovers too.

Serves 4 ■ prep 5 mins

leftover chicken biryani, chilled (about 600g/1lb 5oz)
2 tbsp mayonnaise
squeeze of lemon juice
Little Gem lettuce and sliced cucumber, to serve

Mix the cold chicken rice with the mayonnaise and the lemon juice and serve with the Little Gem leaves and some sliced cucumber.

Per serving: 264 kcalories, protein 16.5g, carbohydrate 27.9g, fat 10.4g, saturated fat 2.4g, fibre 0.7g, sugar 6.5g, salt 0.86g

Fragrant roast chicken

A roast doesn't have to be confined to Sundays. All you need is 10 minutes in the kitchen, then you can leave the bird in the oven while you tick off a few other tasks.

1   Heat oven to 200C/fan 180C/gas 6. Put half a lemon and half a garlic bulb into the chicken's cavity, then put the chicken into a roasting tin. Mix the butter, crushed garlic and half the spices and spread over the chicken breast and legs. Season well.

2   Put the remaining garlic bulbs into the tin and roast the chicken for 1 hour. Mix the remaining spices into the yogurt and season.

3   Remove the chicken from the oven and smother with the yogurt. Spoon over some of the juices, add the remaining lemon to the tin, then roast for 15 mins or until the yogurt is golden and set, and the juices run clear. Lift the chicken on to a board, cover and rest for 10 mins before carving. Serve hot or cold.

Per serving: 379 kcalories, protein 29g, carbohydrate 3g, fat 28g, saturated fat 12g, fibre none, sugar 2g, salt 1.96g

TIP The chicken can be prepared up to a day ahead (to the end of step 1) and kept uncooked and covered in the fridge.

Serves 6 ■ prep 10 mins ■ cook 1¼ hours

1 large chicken, about 1.8kg/4lb
2 lemons, halved
2 garlic bulbs, halved across the middle, plus 2 garlic cloves, crushed
50g/2oz butter, softened
2 tsp *Ras el hanout* spice mix
1 tsp smoked paprika (optional)
200g pot Greek yogurt
(there are always leftovers after a roast. Remove all the remaining chicken from the carcass and keep it in the fridge then use to make one of the following four recipes. Use the carcass to make a stock, see page 206)

Chicken and mushroom spud pies

This warming dish is great for using up the smaller, less desirable pieces of chicken after a roast.

Serves 4 ▪ prep 10 mins
▪ cook 20 mins

4 large baking potatoes
2 tsp sunflower oil
250g pack chestnut mushrooms, quartered
1 tsp cornflour
100ml/3½fl oz milk, plus 3 tbsp
leftover cooked skinless chicken, roughly shredded (about 200g/8oz)
handful of fresh parsley, chopped

1   Microwave the potatoes for 10 mins on High, turning after 5 mins, and heat oven to 220C/fan 200C/gas 7. Meanwhile, heat the oil in a frying pan, then fry the mushrooms over a high heat until golden. Stir in the cornflour, gradually adding 100ml of milk, then simmer, stirring, to make a smooth sauce. Season to taste, then stir in the chicken and parsley.

2   Scoop most of the potato from the skins, then mash with the remaining milk and some seasoning. Spoon the chicken filling into the shells, top with the mash, then bake for 10 mins until golden and the skins have crisped a little. Serve with green veg or a salad.

Per serving: 300 kcalories, protein 20.8g, carbohydrate 41.9g, fat 6.7g, saturated fat 1.9g, fibre 3.7g, sugar 3.2g, salt 0.19g

No-cook chicken couscous

A quick, cheap meal that can be thrown together in minutes.

Serves 4 ▪ prep 15–25 mins.

200g/8oz couscous
200g/8oz frozen peas
400ml/14fl oz chicken or vegetable stock
leftover cooked chicken, shredded (about 200g/8oz)
2 large tomatoes, chopped
2 tbsp olive oil, plus extra to drizzle
large squeeze lemon juice

1   Tip the couscous into a heatproof bowl with the peas. Pour over the hot stock, cover with a plate to keep in the heat, and soak for 5 mins.

2   Toss together the chicken, couscous and tomatoes, then drizzle over the olive oil and lemon juice. Season to your taste – you probably won't need to add any salt, just some freshly ground black pepper. Divide between four plates and top with the rest of the chicken strips. Drizzle over a little extra olive oil, to serve.

Per serving: 319 kcalories, protein 23.7g, carbohydrate 33g, fat 11.2g, saturated fat 2.3g, fibre 3.4g, sugar 4.1g, salt 0.63g

Roast chicken wraps

A delicious, healthy twist on Peking duck.

1 Heat the grill to high. Mix the chicken with half of the hoisin sauce so that it's coated, then spread out in an ovenproof dish and grill until sizzling. Warm the tortillas under the grill or according to the pack instructions.

2 Spread the tortillas with the rest of the hoisin sauce, then use to wrap up the chicken, cucumber, onions and watercress. Cut in half and enjoy while still warm.

Per serving: 275 kcalories, protein 19g, carbohydrate 35.7g, fat 7.2g, saturated fat 1.8g, fibre 2.1g, sugar 12.8g, salt 2.40g

Serves 4 ■ prep 5 mins ■ cook 5 mins

leftover cooked skinless chicken, cut into strips (about 200g/8oz)
8 tbsp hoisin sauce
4 flour tortillas
1 cucumber, deseeded and shredded
8 spring onions, trimmed and finely shredded
large handful of watercress

Crunchy chicken salad

A spicy, zesty idea for leftover chicken and a few storecupboard essentials.

Serves 4 ■ prep 5 mins ■ cook 10–12 mins

leftover cooked chicken (about 200g/8oz)
2 tsp mild or medium curry powder
6 tbsp olive oil
4 tbsp mango chutney
juice 1 lemon
1 cucumber, chopped
100g/4oz watercress
4 tbsp flaked almonds, toasted

1 Toss the chicken with the curry powder and 1 tbsp of the oil. Heat a large non-stick pan and warm the chicken until heated through, then cut into strips.

2 Whisk the remaining oil and mango chutney with a good squeeze of lemon juice. Then, in a large bowl, toss with the cucumber, watercress, chicken and most of the flaked almonds. Divide between four bowls, scatter with the rest of the almonds, and enjoy with some crusty bread on the side.

Per serving: 346 kcalories, protein 17.4g, carbohydrate 10g, fat 26.5g, saturated fat 4g, fibre 2.2g, sugar 8.6g, salt 0.67g

Garlic beef

The cheaper cut of meat used here can be griddled or barbecued and becomes especially tender when marinated beforehand.

Serves 4 ▪ prep 10 mins, plus marinating ▪ cook 15 mins

1½ tbsp black peppercorns
8 garlic cloves
6 tbsp red wine vinegar
800g/1lb 12oz piece well-trimmed
   beef skirt
(reserve about 200g/8oz of
cooked beef to make one of the
following the leftover ideas)

1   In a pestle and mortar, crush the peppercorns and garlic with a pinch of salt until you have a smooth paste, then stir in the vinegar. Sit the beef in a non-metallic dish, then rub all over with the paste. Leave in the fridge for a few hours, but no longer.

2   To cook, place a griddle pan over a very hot heat. Rub the marinade off the meat, then season with a little more salt. Cook the meat until charred on each side – about 5 mins each side for rare. If the cut is very thick, you can roast it in the oven (preheated to 220C/fan 200C/gas 7) for 5 mins after searing.

3   Lift on to a chopping board, then rest for 5 mins before carving into slices and serving with chips, if you like.

Per serving: 190 kcalories, protein 30.3g, carbohydrate 4.5g, fat 5.7g, saturated fat 2.3g, fibre 0.3g, sugar 0.3g, salt 0.19g

Beef tabbouleh

Bulghar wheat has more bite than couscous, but you can use couscous in the recipe instead.

Serves 4 ■ prep 35 mins

200g/8oz bulghar wheat
leftover cooked beef, shredded
  (about 200g/8oz)
4 fresh mint leaves, torn
large handful fresh coriander,
  chopped
2 handfuls cherry tomatoes,
  halved
juice 2 limes
splash of fish sauce

Soak the bulghar wheat for 30 mins in hot water. Drain well, then mix with the shredded beef, the mint, chopped coriander and halved cherry tomatoes. Stir in the lime juice and a splash of fish sauce and serve.

Per serving: 265 kcalories, protein 20.8g, carbohydrate 39.1g, fat 3.9g, saturated fat 1.4g, fibre 0.2g, sugar 1.5g, salt 0.26g

Beef strips with crunchy Thai salad

You can warm the beef strips for this, if you prefer.

Serves 4 ■ prep 5 mins

6 tbsp fresh lime juice
Splash of fish sauce
1 tbsp light muscovado sugar
½ red chilli, deseeded and finely
  chopped
200g/8oz salad leaves
100g/4oz carrots, grated
handful beansprouts
leftover cooked beef, sliced
  (about 200g/8oz)

1   Mix together the lime juice, fish sauce, sugar and chilli in a jug. Tip the salad, carrot and beansprouts into a bowl, then add the dressing, tossing everything together. Divide among four plates.

2   Toss the sliced beef through the salad and serve. Steamed rice flavoured with rice vinegar makes a good acccompaniment.

Per serving: 121 kcalories, protein 16.3g, carbohydrate 7.1g, fat 3.3g, saturated fat 1.3g, fibre 1.1g, sugar 6.9g, salt 0.26g

Asian beef salad

A speedy way to spice up a mid-week salad.

1 Soak the rice noodles according to the pack instructions and drain. Whisk together the soy sauce, lime, ginger and oil in a large serving bowl.

2 Add the beef to the bowl along with the remaining ingredients and the noodles. Toss everything together, then serve.

Per serving: 401 kcalories, protein 20.2g, carbohydrate 57.6g, fat 11.7g, saturated fat 2.4g, fibre 1.6g, sugar 6.1g, salt 1.49g

Serves 4 ■ prep 15 mins ■ cook 10 mins

250g pack rice noodles
2–3 tbsp soy sauce
juice 1 lime
knob root ginger, peeled and grated
3 tbsp olive oil
leftover cooked beef, sliced (about 200g/8oz)
2 red peppers, deseeded and chopped
1 cucumber, chopped
handful fresh coriander leaves, chopped

Cold roast beef with beetroot salad and horseradish cream

A timeless classic that makes a simple supper or stylish starter.

1 To make the horseradish cream, whisk all the ingredients together with salt and freshly ground black pepper until spoonable, then set aside. Lay the slices of beef on four serving plates. In a bowl, mix together the beetroot, shallot and salad leave. Dress with the sherry vinegar and 3 tbsp of the olive oil, then gently toss.

2 Neatly pile a mound of salad over the beef and scatter some of the smallest leaves around the outside. Top the salad with a neat spoonful of horseradish cream, drizzle with the remaining olive oil and serve.

Per serving: 301 kcalories, protein 17.8g, carbohydrate 5.9g, fat 23.1g, saturated fat 7.1g, fibre 2.1g, sugar 4.9g, salt 0.19g

Serves 4 ■ prep 20 mins

leftover cooked beef, sliced (about 200g/8oz)
3 small cooked beetroot, chopped into thin matchsticks
1 shallot, finely chopped
4 handfuls salad leaves, such as frisée and watercress
1 tbsp sherry vinegar
5 tbsp olive oil
For the horseradish cream
5 tbsp fresh horseradish, grated
4 tbsp crème fraîche
pinch of mustard powder
juice ½ lemon

chapter 3

Budget family dinners

It's sometimes difficult to come up with new and inspiring ideas to feed the family every week. We've pulled together plenty of interesting recipes for you to cook that use everyday ingredients and we have kept an eye on the price, so you can be sure that each meal comes in cheaply without compromising on taste.

The majority of the recipes featured in this cookbook use inexpensive ingredients, but this chapter in particular focuses on a selection of ideas that specifically use cheap ingredients to create balanced, filling meals.

There are lots of simple ways to cut cooking costs without sacrificing flavour. Use cheaper cuts of meat such as chicken thighs rather than breast meat; lamb or pork chops rather than steaks. Some meat is cheaper than others but tastes just as good, like turkey, which makes a good substitute for more costly chicken. Bulk out soups and stews with pasta, pulses and rice, or turn a salad into a hearty meal by adding couscous.

Equally, if a dish calls for cod, look out for other firm, white fish offered at a better price and use it in the recipe instead.

Look out for supermarket own-brands and 'basic' ranges, which are often just as good as more recognized brands but have less exciting and enticing packaging. Finally, look out for special offers – if they are good, buy two and freeze one for later in the month. The savings you make from careful shopping can be spent on free-range produce and the rest can stay in your purse for next time.

Budget know-how

■ The trick to cooking inexpensive meals during the week is being a clever shopper. Think about the meals you will actually have time to make, not the meals you would like to do if you had more time, and shop accordingly.

■ Use meat less often; it's the most expensive item on many people's shopping list and protein can be found in many other ways — fish or pulses, for example, are reasonably priced alternatives.

■ When buying meat, look for cheaper cuts. Of course, if less-popular cuts start to sell well, prices will go up and the expensive cuts will become cheaper! Remember to keep cross checking to see what is currently the best deal.

■ Our recipes don't take into consideration current offers in the supermarket, so adapt them to use ingredients that are on offer. Pick the sausages that are the best deal, even if we've suggested a particular flavour, and choose the fish that is the best price when you make your purchase, for example.

Mexican tuna and bean salad

A fresh and spicy treat. Leftovers make a great packed lunch.

1   Toast the pitta breads. Once cool, tear into large pieces.

2   Mix together the beans, avocados, tomatoes, spring onions and chilli. Flake the tuna on top of the salad, pour over the French dressing, then add the crisp pieces of pitta. Mix gently and serve straight away.

Per serving: 820 kcalories, protein 55g, carbohydrate 83g, fat 32g, saturated fat 4g, fibre 15g, sugar 15g, salt 3.18g

TIP Make your own salad dressing by mixing 3 tbsp olive oil with a squeeze of fresh lemon juice, then season to taste.

Serves 4 ■ prep 10 mins

4 large pitta breads
2 × 410g can mixed beans, drained and rinsed
2 avocados, peeled and chopped
6 large tomatoes, deseeded and chopped
bunch spring onions, chopped
1 red chilli, deseeded and chopped
2 × 200g cans tuna in water, drained
5–6 tbsp French dressing, homemade or bought

Minty lamb with warm veg salad

The quick mint sauce brings the ingredients in this dish together nicely for a simple midweek meal.

1   Heat oven to 220C/fan 200C/gas 7. Mix together the carrots, parsnips and onions in a roasting tin with 1 tbsp of the oil, then roast for 15 mins. Toss in the beetroot, drizzle with 2 tbsp of the balsamic vinegar, then roast for 15 mins more until just tender.

2   Meanwhile, heat 1 tbsp of the oil in a non-stick frying pan. Fry the chops for 6–8 mins, turning over after 3–4 mins, until cooked to your liking. Whizz half the mint in a small food processor with the remaining vinegar and a dash of oil, then season. Add a little water if the mixture is a bit thick. Toss the remaining mint with the roasted veg, then season and serve alongside the chops, drizzled with mint sauce.

Per serving: 398 kcalories, protein 30g, carbohydrate 33g, fat 17g, saturated fat 6g, fibre 9g, sugar 24g, salt 0.51g

Serves 4 ■ prep 10 mins
■ cook 30 mins

3 carrots, peeled and chopped into sticks
3 medium parsnips, peeled and chopped into sticks
2 red onions, peeled and chopped into wedges
2 tbsp olive oil, plus extra for mint sauce
3 large cooked beetroot, chopped into wedges
3 tbsp balsamic vinegar
4 lamb chops, trimmed
small bunch fresh mint, roughly chopped

Warm mushroom, lentil and goat's cheese salad ❄

As this warm autumnal salad gives you three of your five-a-day veg, you could serve it with a glass of fruit juice, follow it with an apple or pear and get your daily requirement in one meal.

Serves 4 ■ prep 15 mins
■ cook 5 mins

3 tbsp olive oil
250g/9oz mushrooms, chopped
2 tbsp red wine vinegar
2 tsp Dijon mustard
2 red peppers, deseeded and
 finely chopped
½ red onion, finely chopped
410g can lentils, drained and
 rinsed
2–3 Little Gem lettuces, leaves
 separated
100g/4oz goat's cheese, crumbled

1   Heat 2 tbsp of the oil in a non-stick frying pan, then quickly fry the mushrooms until just starting to soften. Remove from the heat, then stir in the remaining oil with the vinegar and mustard. Stir well until mixed, then add the peppers, onion and lentils, and mix well again.

2   Arrange the leaves over four plates. Spoon the lentil salad over the top, add the goat's cheese and serve.

Per serving: 220 kcalories, protein 10g, carbohydrate 15g, fat 14g, saturated fat 4g, fibre 4g, sugar 7g, salt 1.31g

Summer couscous salad

A delicious Middle Eastern meal in minutes.

1 Tip the couscous into a bowl, pour over the boiling stock and mix well with a fork. Cover with a plate and leave for 4 mins. Tip all the dressing ingredients into a bowl and mix well. Fluff up the couscous with a fork, stir in the chickpeas and follow with half the dressing. Mix well and pile on to a large serving dish.

2 Heat 1 tbsp of oil in a large frying pan and fry the courgette over a high heat for 2–3 mins until dark golden brown. Lift out on to kitchen paper. Now put the tomatoes cut-side down into the pan, and cook for another couple of mins until tinged brown on the underside. Top the couscous with the courgettes and the tomatoes.

3 If the pan is dry, pour in a little more oil, then add the halloumi strips and fry for 2–3 mins, turning them over from time to time, until crisp and golden brown. Pile on top of the tomatoes, and drizzle with the remaining dressing. Serve immediately.

Per serving: 721 kcalories, protein 23g, carbohydrate 47g, fat 50g, saturated fat 14g, fibre 4g, sugar 1g, salt 2.86g

Serves 4 ■ prep 10 mins
■ cook 20–25 mins

250g/9oz couscous
250ml/9fl oz vegetable stock
410g can chickpeas, drained and rinsed
1–2 tbsp vegetable or olive oil
300g/10oz courgettes, chopped
300g/10oz small vine-ripened tomatoes, halved
250g pack halloumi, sliced into strips
for the dressing
125ml/4fl oz olive oil
3 tbsp lime juice
2 large garlic cloves, finely chopped
2 tbsp fresh mint, chopped
½ tsp sugar

Coriander cod with carrot pilaf

Any firm white fish will do for this dish.

**Serves 4 ■ prep 8 mins
■ cook 12–15 mins**

2 tbsp olive oil
4 skinless cod fillets, each about
    175g/6oz
2 tbsp fresh coriander leaves,
    chopped
zest and juice 1 lemon
1 onion, chopped
2 tsp cumin seeds
2 large carrots, grated
200g/8oz basmati rice
600ml/1 pint vegetable stock

1   Heat the grill pan to high, then line with double-thickness foil and curl up the edges to catch the juices. Brush lightly with oil and put the cod on top. Sprinkle over the coriander, lemon zest and juice, and drizzle with a little more of the oil. Season with salt and pepper, then grill for 10–12 mins until the fish flakes easily.

2   Meanwhile, heat the remaining oil in a pan. Add the onion and cumin, and fry for a few mins. Add the carrots and stir well, then stir in the rice until glistening. Add the stock and bring to the boil. Cover and cook gently for about 10 mins until the rice is tender and the stock absorbed. Spoon the rice on to four warm plates, top with the cod and pour over the pan juices.

Per serving: 305 kcalories, protein 14g, carbohydrate 50g, fat 7g, saturated fat 1g, fibre 3g, sugar 8g, salt 0.31g

Sticky chicken with mango couscous

Couscous is the perfect partner for this fruity glazed chicken.

**Serves 4 ■ prep 10 mins
■ cook 10 mins**

1 large mango
4 spring onions, chopped
1 heaped tsp ground cumin
3 tbsp white wine vinegar
250g/9oz couscous
3 tbsp thick-cut marmalade
4 tsp wholegrain mustard
4 skinless chicken breasts, each
    chopped into 3–4 strips

1   Heat the grill to high. Peel and dice the mango, toss with most of the spring onions, and the cumin and rice vinegar, then set aside. Put the couscous in a large heatproof bowl, pour over 400ml boiling water, then cover with cling film and set aside.

2   Mix the marmalade and mustard. Lay the chicken strips in a roasting tin, then brush over half of the marmalade glaze. Grill for 4–5 mins, then turn the chicken over and brush with the remaining glaze. Grill for a further 4–5 mins until the chicken is cooked through and the glaze is bubbling. The couscous should then be ready. Stir in the mango mixture and serve with the hot chicken strips and the remaining spring onions sprinkled over.

Per serving: 368 kcalories, protein 35.1g, carbohydrate 53.4g, fat 3.1g, saturated fat 0.6g, fibre 2.7g, sugar 21.2g, salt 0.43g

TIP Swap the marmalade for 3 tbsp clear honey and drizzle over 8 good-quality chipolatas on a baking sheet. Grill for 10 mins, turning occasionally, until the sausages are browned and sticky. Serve with the mango couscous as before.

Spiced sweet potato salad with crisp noodles

An easy, flavour-packed way to make the most of this versatile veg.

Serves 4 ▪ prep 5 mins
▪ cook 25 mins

4 medium sweet potatoes, peeled
  and chopped into chunks
2 tsp cumin seeds
4 tsp sunflower oil, plus extra for
  frying
50g/2oz dried fine egg noodles
zest and juice 1 orange
3 tsp red wine vinegar
4 handfuls spinach leaves
1 avocado, peeled and chopped
½ red onion, finely chopped

1　Heat oven to 200C/fan 180C/gas 6. Toss the potato chunks with the cumin, 2 tsp of the oil and some seasoning. Spread over a baking sheet, then roast for 20–25 mins until tender and golden.

2　Meanwhile, cook the noodles according to the pack instructions, then drain. Heat 1cm of oil in a wok until a piece of noodle dropped in begins to sizzle immediately. Fry the noodles in batches for 30 secs until crisp. Remove and drain on kitchen paper.

3　When the potatoes are ready, whisk together the remaining 1tsp oil with the orange zest and juice and the red wine vinegar, and season. Gently mix the sweet potatoes, spinach, avocado, red onion and dressing in a bowl. Divide among four plates and crumble over the crispy noodles.

Per serving: 411 kcalories, protein 7g, carbohydrate 47g, fat 23g, saturated fat 3g, fibre 8g, sugar 13g, salt 0.41g

TIP　To check that an avocado is ripe, press gently at the ends; it should give slightly under your touch. Avocados can turn bad from the inside out, and they bruise easily so take care when handling them and use as soon as they are ripe. An under-ripe avocado will ripen if left in the fruit bowl for a day or so.

Quick veg and soft cheese frittata

Eggs are a fantastic weekday staple, as they can be whipped up into any number of meals in minutes.

1 In a large non-stick frying pan, fry the lardons in the oil until starting to brown. Add the courgettes, then fry for a couple of mins until they begin to soften. Add the sweetcorn and spinach, season to taste, then heat through.

2 Heat the grill to medium. Beat the eggs then pour over the vegetables. Crumble over the cheese, then cook gently on the hob until the egg has just set around the edges, about 5 mins. Slide the frittata under the grill, then cook until the egg is set and the top is lightly browned. Cut into wedges and serve with a green salad.

Per serving: 540 kcalories, protein 29g, carbohydrate 18g, fat 40g, saturated fat 16g, fibre 4g, sugar 5g, salt 1.62g

Serves 4 ■ prep 10 mins, plus defrosting ■ cook 20 mins

100g/4oz lardons
1 tbsp olive oil
2 large courgettes, chopped into chunks
350g/12oz frozen sweetcorn, defrosted
400g/14oz frozen spinach, defrosted and drained
8 eggs
150g pack soft cheese with garlic and herbs

Pan-fried salmon with tabbouleh

Couscous is virtually no-cook and goes well with fish, meat or chicken. It's an ideal alternative to rice and pasta.

1 Put the couscous in a large bowl. Pour over the boiling water or stock and stir. Cover and leave to stand for about 4–5 mins until all the liquid has been absorbed.

2 Meanwhile, heat 1 tbsp of the oil in a frying pan. Add the salmon, skin-side down then fry, without disturbing, for 5–6 mins until golden. Turn, leave for 1–2 mins, then take the pan off the heat. Leave for 1 min more to finish cooking in the heat from the pan.

3 Fluff up the couscous with a fork. Add the tomatoes, cucumber, spring onion, parsley, and lemon zest. Whisk the remaining olive oil, lemon juice and crushed garlic with plenty of seasoning, drizzle over the couscous and toss. Serve with the salmon.

Per serving: 320 kcalories, protein 5g, carbohydrate 37g, fat 18g, saturated fat 3g, fibre 2g, sugar none, salt 0.04g

KNOW-HOW Salmon freezes well. Try frozen fish too. It's often fresher than the fish counter or pre-packed. You'll find more sustainable choices at a decent price.

Serves 4 ■ prep 10 mins ■ cook 8–10 mins

250g/9oz couscous
250ml/9fl oz boiling water or stock
7 tbsp olive oil
4 salmon fillets
4 tomatoes, finely chopped
½ cucumber, finely chopped
bunch spring onions, chopped
large handful fresh parsley leaves, finely chopped
zest and juice 1 lemon
1 garlic clove, crushed

Really easy beefburgers

Add a slice of mild cheddar to each of these before lifting them out of the griddle pan if you want to turn them into cheeseburgers.

Serves 4 ▪ prep 30 mins ▪ cook 35 mins

500g pack lean minced beef
1 tsp mild chilli powder
for the buns and toppings
4 burger baps
mayonnaise/ketchup, or both
choice of lettuce leaves, tomato, cucumber, gherkin and red onion, chopped

1 Put the mince in a mixing bowl with the chilli powder and a little salt and pepper. Mix well with your hands, and divide the mixture into four, then shape into round burgers.

2 Cook the burgers in a hot griddle pan for 5 mins each side, turning carefully. When the burgers are ready, cut the burger baps in half and warm them in the toaster.

3 Spread a little mayonnaise or ketchup (or both) on the cut side of each toasted bun half, then top with the burgers and salad selection, followed by the remaining half buns.

Per serving: 496 kcalories, protein 39g, carbohydrate 26g, fat 27g, saturated fat 12g, fibre 1g, sugar 2g, salt 1.53g

Aubergine and tomato grill

This takes less than half an hour to make and is delicious with a green salad.

Serves 4 ▪ prep 10 mins ▪ cook 15 mins

4 medium aubergines
2 tbsp olive oil
2 small onions or 1 large one, chopped
2 x 400g cans chopped tomatoes
175g/6oz low-fat soft cheese with garlic and herbs
6 tbsp breadcrumbs

1 Trim the stalks from the aubergines, then cut each into six slices lengthways. Lay them in one layer on a grill pan and lightly brush with oil and a little seasoning. Grill until lightly browned, turn them over, brush with oil again, then grill until browned and tender (you may have to do this in batches).

2 Heat the remaining oil in a non-stick pan, add the onion and gently fry until softened. Add the tomatoes and simmer for 5 mins. When the aubergines are cool, spread half the slices with a little soft cheese and cover with the remaining slices to make sandwiches.

3 Spread half the tomato sauce over a shallow ovenproof dish. Arrange the aubergine sandwiches, overlapping, on top and pour over the remaining sauce. Sprinkle over the crumbs, then grill until browned.

Per serving: 272 kcalories, protein 10.2g, carbohydrate 28.3g, fat 13.9g, saturated fat 5.1g, fibre 7.9g, sugar 12.8g, salt 1.21g

Superhealthy salmon burgers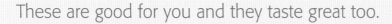

These are good for you and they taste great too.

1   Tip the salmon into a food processor with the curry paste, ginger, soy sauce and chopped coriander. Pulse until roughly minced. Tip out the mix and shape into four burgers. Heat the oil in a non-stick frying pan, then fry the burgers for 4–5 mins each side, turning until crisp and cooked through.

2   Meanwhile, using a vegetable peeler, peel strips of carrot and cucumber into a bowl. Toss with the vinegar and sugar until the sugar has dissolved, then mix through the coriander leaves. Divide the salad among four plates. Serve with the burgers and some rice, with lemon wedges on the side.

Per serving: 292 kcalories, protein 29g, carbohydrate 7g, fat 17g, saturated fat 4g, fibre 2g, sugar 6g, salt 0.83g

Serves 4 ■ prep 20 mins ■ cook 10 mins

4 boneless, skinless salmon fillets (about 550g/1lb 4oz in total, cut into chunks)
2 tbsp Thai red curry paste
thumb-size piece root ginger, grated
1 tsp soy sauce
bunch fresh coriander, half chopped, half leaves picked
1 tsp vegetable oil
lemon wedges, to serve
for the salad
2 carrots
½ large or 1 small cucumber
2 tbsp white wine vinegar
1 tsp caster sugar

Spiced turkey burgers

Turkey is low in fat and inexpensive, so it's ideal for midweek meals.

1   In a large bowl, mix the turkey mince, the onion, garlic, curry powder, coriander and the egg yolk with a little salt and pepper. Combine well with your hands, then shape into four flat burgers.

2   Heat the oil in a frying pan over a high heat, then cook the burgers for 5 mins on each side or until cooked through. Toast the cut sides of the burger buns. Put the salad on the bottom halves of the warm buns, then top with the burgers and chutney or lime pickle, and cap with the top halves of the buns.

Per serving: 318 kcalories, protein 34g, carbohydrate 26g, fat 9g, saturated fat 2g, fibre 2g, sugar 2g, salt 0.95g

Serves 4 ■ prep 10 mins ■ cook 10 mins

500g/1lb 2oz turkey mince
½ red onion, finely chopped
1 garlic clove, crushed
2 tsp Madras curry powder
handful fresh coriander leaves, chopped
1 egg yolk
1 tbsp sunflower oil
for the buns and topping
4 burger buns
salad and mango chutney or lime pickle, to serve

Baked haddock and cabbage risotto

A comforting and filling rice one-pot.

1   Heat oven to 200C/fan 180C/gas 6. Heat the oil in a 2-litre casserole dish, then soften the onion over a medium heat for about 5 mins. Tip in the rice and cook for 2 mins, stirring well. Pour in the stock, bring to the boil, then add the cabbage. Cover and bake for 20 mins.

2   Remove the pan from the oven and give the rice a stir. Put the fish on top of the rice, replace the lid, then bake for 5 mins.

3   Flake the fish into large chunks and stir into the rice with the crème fraîche and half the parmesan. Season with freshly ground black pepper, then sprinkle with the remaining parmesan to serve.

Per serving: 469 kcalories, protein 32g, carbohydrate 66g, fat 10g, saturated fat 4g, fibre 5g, sugar 7g, salt 2.52g

KNOW-HOW Retailers are still lagging behind when it comes to accurate labelling, so to be sure that you're buying sustainable supplies, regularly check the Marine Stewardship Council's website (msc.org) or look out for their tick on packs.

Serves 4 ■ prep 5 mins ■ cook 35 mins

1 tbsp olive oil
1 onion, chopped
300g/10oz risotto rice
1 litre/1¾ pints fish or vegetable stock
300g/10oz wedge Savoy cabbage, chopped
400g/14oz skinless smoked haddock
3 tbsp half-fat crème fraîche
50g/2oz parmesan, grated

Red-spiced fish with green salad

The delicate Thai taste of this dish is a good introduction to spicy food for children.

1   Heat oven to 200C/fan 180C/gas 6. Brush each fillet with 1 tsp of the paste and roast on a baking sheet for 8–10 mins until the fish flakes easily.

2   Meanwhile, mix the rest of the ingredients in a large bowl with some seasoning. Serve with the Thai spiced fish and a scoop of rice.

Per serving: 209 kcalories, protein 24.2g, carbohydrate 3.9g, fat 10.8g, saturated fat 1.6g, fibre 2.3g, sugar 3.2g, salt 0.60g

TIP Try Thai green or yellow curry paste, or give this dish an Indian kick with some tikka paste.

Serves 4 ■ prep 10 mins ■ cook 10 mins

4 fillets white fish, like hake
4 tsp Thai red curry paste
1 avocado, chopped
1 cucumber, halved lengthways, deseeded and chopped
2 Little Gem lettuces, leaves torn
small bunch fresh coriander leaves, chopped
zest and juice 1 lime
1 tsp clear honey

Hob-to-table moussaka ❄

Try this quick variation on the Greek classic that still makes a rich and hearty one-pot.

Serves 4 ■ prep 10 mins ■ cook 25 mins

2 tbsp olive oil
1 large onion, finely chopped
2 garlic cloves, finely chopped
500g/1lb 2oz minced lamb
400g can chopped plum tomatoes
2 tbsp tomato purée
2 tsp ground cinnamon
200g jar chargrilled aubergines in olive oil, drained and chopped
200g pack feta, crumbled
3 tbsp fresh mint, chopped

1   Heat the oil in a large, shallow pan. Toss in the onion and garlic, and fry until soft. Add the mince and stir-fry for 3–4 mins until browned.

2   Tip the tomatoes into the pan and stir in the tomato purée and cinnamon, then season generously with salt and pepper. Leave the mince to simmer for 20 mins, adding the aubergines half-way through.

3   To serve, sprinkle the crumbled feta and mint over the mince. Bring the moussaka to the table as the feta melts and serve with a crunchy green salad and toasted pitta.

Per serving: 529 kcalories, protein 35g, carbohydrate 11g, fat 39g, saturated fat 16g, fibre 3g, added sugar none, salt 2.31g

Creamy egg curry

This dish may sound like an unusual combination of ingredients, but trust us it works.

Serves 4 ■ prep 10 mins ■ cook 20 mins

2 tbsp sunflower oil
2 onions, finely chopped
2 heaped tbsp curry paste (we used Tikka Masala)
400g can chopped tomatoes
8 eggs
140g/5oz frozen peas
4 tbsp Greek yogurt
rice and mango chutney, to serve

1   Heat the oil in a pan, then fry the onion over a low heat for 10 mins until golden. Add the curry paste and sizzle for 2 mins, stirring. Add the tomatoes and 200ml of water, season to taste then bring to the boil. Simmer for 10 mins until you have a rich sauce.

2   Meanwhile, boil the eggs for 8 mins, cool in cold water, then peel and halve.

3   Stir the peas and yogurt into the curry, and simmer for another 2–3 mins. Add the eggs, spoon over the curry sauce and leave for another 2 mins to heat through. Serve with rice and mango chutney.

Per serving: 336 kcalories, protein 20g, carbohydrate 11g, fat 24g, saturated fat 5g, fibre 3g, sugar 7g, salt 1.02g

Green garden veg pie

Just put this healthy veggie dish in the middle of the table and watch everyone dive in.

Serves 4 ■ prep 15 mins ■ cook 35 mins

50g/2oz butter
50g/2oz plain flour
2 tsp mustard powder
600ml/1pint milk
200g/8oz mature cheddar, grated
2 large potatoes, chopped into rounds
1 head broccoli, chopped into little florets
1 head cauliflower, chopped into little florets
200g/8oz frozen peas
small bunch fresh chives, snipped

1   Melt the butter in a pan, then stir in the flour and mustard powder, and cook for 1 min. Gradually stir in the milk until smooth with no lumps, then keep stirring until the mixture begins to bubble and thickens to a creamy sauce. Remove from the heat, then stir in all but a handful of the grated cheese.

2   Heat oven to 220C/fan 200C/gas 7. Bring a large pan of water to the boil, and cook the potato slices for 5 mins. Tip in the broccoli and cauliflower for another 3 mins, then add the peas for 1 more min. Drain all the veg and pat dry. Reserve enough potato slices to cover the top of the finished dish, then gently stir the rest of the vegetables into the sauce with the chives.

3   Tip into a deep ovenproof dish, arrange over the reserved potato slices, then sprinkle with the remaining cheddar. Bake for 20–25 mins until the topping is golden and crisp, then serve straight from the dish.

Per serving: 604 kcalories, protein 33g, carbohydrate 45g, fat 34g, saturated fat 19g, fibre 9g, sugar 14g, salt 1.34g

Bacon and broccoli pasta

With a few basic ingredients you can have a tasty and colourful supper in no time.

Serves 4 ■ prep 5 mins ■ cook 15 mins

500g pack dried pasta (we used farfalle)
1 broccoli head (about 300g/10oz) chopped into small florets
8 rashers rindless smoked bacon
5 tbsp pesto
grated parmesan, to serve

1   Cook the pasta according to the pack instructions. About 3 mins before the pasta is cooked, throw in the broccoli. When everything is done, drain, reserving about 100ml of the cooking water.

2   While the pasta is cooking, grill the bacon for 6–7 mins until crisp, then cut into bite-sized pieces. Add the bacon and pesto to the pasta pan, toss together well and loosen with a little of the cooking water, if needed. Sprinkle over the parmesan and serve.

Per serving 655 kcalories, protein 32g, carbohydrates 96g, fat 18g, saturated fat 6g, fibre 6g, sugar 4g, salt 2.72g

Chicken and leek pot pies

This can make one big pie, if you prefer. Use a 1.2-litre pie dish and increase the cooking time in the oven by about 10 minutes.

1   Heat oven to 200C/fan 180C/gas 6. Boil the potatoes and parsnips for 15 mins until tender. Drain, reserving the water, then mash with a little seasoning. Set aside.

2   Toss the chicken in the cornflour. Heat the oil in a large pan, add the leeks, then fry for 3 mins until starting to soften. Add the chicken and 200ml of water from the potatoes, then bring to the boil, stirring. Reduce the heat, then gently simmer for 10 mins, until the chicken is just tender. Remove from the heat, then stir in the lemon zest, parsley, crème fraîche and mustard.

3   Divide the chicken filling among four 300ml pie dishes. Spoon over the mash and spread roughly with a fork to seal in the filling. Bake for 25 mins until the topping is crisp and golden.

Per serving: 331 kcalories, protein 36g, carbohydrate 34g, fat 7g, saturated fat 1g, fibre 9g, sugar 10g, salt 0.25g

Serves 4 ▪ prep 45 mins
▪ cook 25 mins

500g/1lb 2oz parsnips, peeled and chopped
300g/10oz floury potatoes, peeled and chopped
500g/1lb 2oz skinless chicken breasts, chopped into small chunks
2 tsp cornflour
1 tbsp olive oil
4 leeks, chopped
zest 1 lemon
2 tbsp fresh parsley, chopped
2 tbsp low-fat crème fraîche
1 tbsp wholegrain mustard

Turkey, thyme and leek meatloaf ❄

There's no need to save turkey for Christmas — it makes a nutritious and cheap midweek meal any time.

1   Heat oven to 220C/fan 200C/gas 7. Heat the oil in a frying pan, then soften the leeks for 5 mins. Line the base of a 28x18cm baking tin with greaseproof paper.

2   Mix the mince, thyme leaves, two thirds of the breadcrumbs, leeks and egg together with a little seasoning, then tip into the tin. Press the mixture firmly into the tin then ruffle the surface with a fork. Mix together the remaining breadcrumbs and bacon and scatter over the top. Cook for 15 mins then finish under the grill until golden and crisp on top. Serve with boiled potatoes and carrots.

Per serving: 300 kcalories, protein 36.9g, carbohydrate 20.9g, fat 8.3g, saturated fat 1.6g, fibre 3.8g, sugar 3.9g, salt 1.03g

Serves 4 ▪ prep 10 mins
▪ cook 20 mins

1 tbsp sunflower oil
4 large leeks, chopped
500g pack turkey mince
2 fresh thyme sprigs, leaves removed
85g/3oz breadcrumbs
1 egg, beaten
2 rashers rindless lean back bacon, fat trimmed, chopped

Gnocchi with roasted squash and goat's cheese

Create a luxurious-tasting dish, with minimal ingredients.

Serves 4 ▪ prep 15 mins ▪ cook 20 mins

450g/1lb butternut squash, peeled and chopped into small chunks
1 garlic clove
2 tbsp olive oil
500g pack fresh potato gnocchi
200g/8oz baby spinach leaves
100g/4oz soft goat's cheese

1 Heat oven to 200C/fan 180C/gas 6. Tip the squash into a roasting tin with the garlic and oil, salt and pepper, and mix well. Roast for 20 mins, shaking the pan halfway through, until tender and golden.

2 Meanwhile, boil the gnocchi according to the pack instructions. With a few seconds to go, throw in the spinach, then drain the gnocchi and spinach together. Tip into the roasting tin, then mix everything together well, mashing the softened garlic. Spoon on to four warm plates, then crumble over the cheese to serve.

Per serving: 333 kcalories, protein 11g, carbohydrate 53g, fat 10g, saturated fat 4g, fibre 5g, sugar 8g, salt 1.76g

Herby turkey meatballs ❄

You can freeze these meatballs in the sauce for a speedy supper.

1   Tip the breadcrumbs into a large bowl and stir in the milk until the crumbs have absorbed all the liquid. Add the mince, 1 tsp of the oregano, half the parsley, a little salt and pepper, and mash together with a fork. Use wet hands to shape into 30 small meatballs.

2   Heat the oil in a large non-stick pan and brown the meatballs for 5 mins, turning to cook all sides. Pour in the passata, sugar, remaining oregano and most of the remaining parsley. Give everything a good stir and simmer gently for 8–10 mins until the meatballs are just cooked through. Cook the pasta according to the pack instructions. Season, then spoon over the pasta and sprinkle over the remaining parsley.

Per serving: 655 kcalories, protein 32g, carbohydrate 96g, fat 18g, saturated fat 6g, fibre 6g, sugar 4g, salt 2.72g

Serves 4 ■ prep 15 mins
■ cook 15 mins

85g/3oz breadcrumbs
75ml/2½fl oz milk
350g/12oz turkey mince
2 tsp dried oregano
small bunch fresh parsley
    leaves, chopped
2 tsp olive oil
680g jar onion and garlic passata
2 tsp sugar
500g bag dried pasta shapes,
    to serve

Rosemary chicken with tomato sauce

Chicken thighs may cost less, but they are packed with flavour.

Serves 4 ▪ prep 5 mins ▪ cook 30 mins

1 tbsp olive oil
8 boneless skinless chicken thighs
1 rosemary sprig, leaves finely chopped
1 red onion, finely chopped
3 garlic cloves, chopped
2 anchovy fillets, chopped
400g can chopped tomatoes
1 tbsp capers, drained
75ml/2½fl oz red wine or water

1   Heat half the oil in a non-stick pan, then brown the chicken all over. Add half the chopped rosemary, stir to coat with oil, then set aside on a plate.

2   In the same pan, heat the rest of the oil, then gently cook the onion for about 5 mins until soft. Add the garlic, anchovies and remaining rosemary, then fry for a few mins more until fragrant. Pour in the tomatoes, capers and the wine or water. Bring to the boil, then return the chicken pieces to the pan. Cover, then cook for 20 mins until the chicken is cooked through. Season and serve with a crisp green salad and crusty bread.

Per serving: 275 kcalories, protein 44g, carbohydrate 5g, fat 9g, saturated fat 3g, fibre 2g, sugar 4g, salt 1.09g

Quick roast lamb

Whip up this relaxed midweek roast. You can easily halve the recipe.

Serves 4 ▪ prep 10 mins ▪ cook 25-30 mins

700g/1lb 9oz new potatoes
500g/1lb 2oz Chantenay carrots, or large carrots cut into big chunks
2 tbsp olive oil, plus a little more for the lamb
2 fresh rosemary sprigs, leaves chopped
150ml/¼ pint red wine
150ml/¼ pint lamb stock
2–3 tsp redcurrant jelly
8 lamb chops or cutlets

1   Heat oven to 220C/fan 200C/gas 7. Divide the potatoes and carrots between two baking sheets, toss with the oil and rosemary, then season well. Roast for 20 mins until the veg is golden and almost tender. You may need to swap the sheets around halfway through.

2   Meanwhile, make the gravy. Put the wine and stock into a small pan, then boil until reduced by about two thirds. Add the redcurrant jelly, season, stir and keep warm.

3   Rub the lamb in a little oil, then season. Tuck the lamb among the veg, then return to the oven for 10 mins, turning the lamb half-way through and swap the sheets round, if necessary. Serve with the redcurrant gravy and some green veg.

Per serving: 606 kcalories, protein 34g, carbohydrate 44g, fat 32g, saturated fat 13g, fibre 5g, sugar 13g, salt 0.7g

Italian tuna balls

A healthy twist on a family favourite.

Serves 4 ▪ prep 15 mins ▪ cook 20 mins

2 × 160g cans tuna in sunflower or olive oil, drained (reserve a little oil)
small handful pine nuts
zest 1 lemon
small handful fresh parsley leaves, roughly chopped
50g/2oz fresh breadcrumbs
1 egg, beaten
400g/14oz spaghetti
500g jar tomato pasta sauce

1 Flake the tuna into a bowl, then tip in the pine nuts, lemon zest, parsley, breadcrumbs and egg. Season and mix together with your hands until completely combined. Roll the mix into 12 walnut-size balls. Put a large pan of salted water on to boil then cook the spaghetti according to the pack instructions.

2 Heat a little of the tuna oil in a large non-stick frying pan, then fry the tuna balls for 5 mins, turning every min or so until completely golden. Drain on kitchen paper. Heat the tomato sauce then toss together with the pasta and tuna balls to serve.

Per serving: 594 kcalories, protein 35g, carbohydrate 92g, fat 12g, saturated fat 2g, fibre 4g, sugar 8g, salt 1.42g

Two-step carbonara

The simple sauce for this dish can be made in the time it takes to boil the pasta.

Serves 4 ▪ prep 2 mins ▪ cook 12 mins

350g/12oz spaghetti or linguine
140g pack diced pancetta or rindless smoked streaky bacon, chopped
2 tsp olive oil
1 garlic clove, crushed
1 egg, plus 4 yolks
50g/2oz parmesan, grated

1 Boil the pasta according to the pack instructions. Meanwhile, in a frying pan, cook the pancetta or bacon in the oil for a few mins until golden and crisp. Add the garlic, fry for 1 min then turn off the heat. Briefly whisk the egg and yolks with most of the parmesan and some seasoning.

2 Drain the pasta, reserving a little of the cooking water. Add the eggs and a tbsp of cooking water, then mix until the pasta is coated and creamy. The heat from the pasta will gently cook the sauce. Stir in the pancetta or bacon and garlic then serve, topped with the remaining parmesan.

Per serving: 575 kcalories, protein 28g, carbohydrate 65g, fat 24g, saturated fat 9g, fibre 3g, sugar 3g, salt 2.11g

20-minute seafood spaghetti

An affordable but smart pasta supper.

1 Heat the oil in a wok or large frying pan, then cook the onion and garlic over a medium heat for 5 mins until soft. Add the paprika, tomatoes and stock, then bring to the boil.

2 Turn down the heat to a simmer, stir in the pasta and cook for 7 mins, stirring occasionally to stop the pasta from sticking. Stir in the seafood, cook for 3 mins more, until it's all heated through and the pasta is cooked, then season to taste. Sprinkle with parsley and serve with lemon wedges.

Per serving: 370 kcalories, protein 23g, carbohydrate 62g, fat 5g, saturated fat 1g, fibre 4g, sugar none, salt 1.4g

Serves 4 ▪ prep 5–10 mins ▪ cook 15 mins

1 tbsp olive oil
1 onion, chopped
1 garlic clove, chopped
1 tsp paprika
400g can chopped tomatoes
1 litre/1¾ pints chicken stock
300g/10oz spaghetti, roughly snapped
240g pack mixed frozen seafood, defrosted
handful fresh parsley leaves, chopped and lemon wedges, to serve

Sausage and tomato pasta ❄

This warming one-pot is sure to please everyone.

1 Heat the olive oil in a heavy-based pan (preferably not non-stick) and add the sausages. Fry for about 8 mins until golden and cooked through. Tip in the garlic and fry for 1 min. Pour in the white wine and boil until it has reduced by half.

2 Stir in the tomato purée and tomatoes, and season to taste. Simmer for 15 mins until the sauce is rich and thick.

3 While the sauce cooks, boil the pasta according to the pack instructions and drain. Stir the basil, if using, and cooked pasta into the sauce, then serve in bowls with grated parmesan.

Per serving: 655 kcalories, protein 24g, carbohydrate 103g, fat 16g, saturated fat 5g, fibre 5g, sugar none, salt 1g

Serves 4 ▪ prep 5 mins ▪ cook 20 mins

1 tbsp olive oil
4 thick pork sausages, cut into bite-size pieces
2 garlic cloves, crushed
200ml/8fl oz white wine
1 tbsp tomato purée
400g can chopped tomatoes
500g pack rigatoni or penne
handful fresh basil leaves, torn (optional)
grated parmesan, to serve

TIP Spice up this dish by adding a pinch of dried chilli or 1 chopped red chilli as you fry the sausages.

Lemon linguine with ham

An easy and inexpensive Italian supper.

Serves 4 ■ prep 2 mins
■ cook 10–12 mins

400g/14oz linguine
cupful of frozen peas
200ml pot crème fraîche
zest ½ lemon and juice
   1 lemon
3–4 slices cooked ham, cut into
   strips

1   Cook the pasta according to the pack instructions, adding the peas for the final 2 mins of cooking.

2   Drain the pasta and return to the pan. Stir in the crème fraîche, lemon zest and juice then season. Serve with the ham strips scattered over.

Per serving: 527 kcalories, protein 24g, carbohydrate 78g, fat 20g, saturated fat 9g, fibre 4g, sugar 4g, salt 0.68g

Creamy courgette lasagne

Making this quick-baked pasta dish means not having to spend lots of time in the kitchen.

Serves 4 ■ prep 10 mins
■ cook 10–15 mins

9 dried lasagne sheets
1 tbsp sunflower oil, plus extra for
   drizzling
1 onion, finely chopped
700g/1lb 9oz courgettes (about 6),
   coarsely grated
2 garlic cloves, crushed
250g pot ricotta
50g/2oz cheddar
350g jar tomato-based pasta sauce

1   Heat oven to 220C/fan 200C/gas 7. Put a pan of water on to boil, then cook the lasagne sheets for about 5 mins until softened but not cooked through. Rinse in cold water, then drizzle with a little oil to stop them sticking together.

2   Meanwhile, heat the oil in a large frying pan, then fry the onion. After 3 mins, add the courgettes and garlic, and continue to fry until the courgette has softened and turned bright green. Stir in two thirds of both the ricotta and the cheddar, then season to taste. Heat the tomato sauce in the microwave for 2 mins on High, or in a pan, until hot.

3   In a large ovenproof baking dish, layer up the lasagne, starting with half the courgette mix, then pasta, then tomato sauce. Repeat, top with blobs of the remaining ricotta, then scatter with the rest of the cheddar. Bake on the top shelf for about 10 mins until the pasta is tender and the cheese is golden.

Per serving: 405 kcalories, protein 18g, carbohydrate 38g, fat 21g, saturated fat 8g, fibre 4g, sugar 13g, salt 1.36g

Sticky green stir-fry with beef

Steak may seem extravagant for midweek, but you can make a meal for four with just two steaks.

Serves 4 ▪ prep 8 mins ▪ cook 12 mins

1 tbsp sunflower oil
2 × 200g/8oz sirloin steaks, trimmed of fat and thinly sliced
1 broccoli head, chopped into small florets
2 garlic cloves, chopped
300g/10oz sugar snap peas
4 spring onions, thickly chopped
3 pak choi, leaves separated and chopped into quarters
4 tbsp hoisin sauce

1 Heat the oil in a large wok or deep frying pan, then sizzle the beef strips for 3–4 mins until browned. Remove and set aside.

2 Toss the broccoli and garlic into the wok with a splash of water, then fry over a high heat for 4–5 mins until starting to soften. Add the peas, spring onions and pak choi. Stir-fry for another 2–3 mins, then stir in the hoisin sauce and beef. Heat through quickly, adding a splash of water if it seems a little dry. Great with noodles or rice.

Per serving: 253 kcalories, protein 32g, carbohydrate 13g, fat 9g, saturated fat 2g, fibre 5g, sugar 10g, salt 0.28g

Easy noodles ❄

This effortless version of a Malaysian dish is microwaved in one bowl.

1   Tip the stock, coconut milk, Thai curry paste, turmeric and chicken into a big microwave-proof bowl. Cover with cling film, pierce it a few times and microwave on High for 5 mins. Remove the cling film, give it a stir and cook for a further 5 mins until the chicken is cooked.

2   Meanwhile, tip the noodles into another large bowl and cover them with boiling water. Leave to soak for 4 mins, then drain.

3   Add the stir-fry mix and noodles to the chicken, ladle into deep bowls and serve with spoons and forks.

Per serving: 516 kcalories, protein 32g, carbohydrate 58g, fat 19g, saturated fat 14g, fibre 1g, sugar none, salt 1.03g

Serves 4 ▪ prep 5 mins ▪ cook 10 mins

- 500ml/18fl oz chicken or vegetable stock
- 400ml can coconut milk (full or reduced fat)
- 1 tbsp Thai green or red curry paste
- 1 tsp turmeric
- 3 skinless chicken breasts, chopped into small chunks
- 250g pack medium rice noodles
- 300g bag stir-fry mix (pick one with beansprouts)

Sweet chilli bangers

Roasting the sausages in a sticky sauce gives them a tasty richness that everyone will love.

Serves 6 ■ prep 5 mins
■ cook 40 mins

12 large pork sausages
4 tbsp tomato ketchup
2 tbsp clear honey
2 tsp mild chilli powder
2 garlic cloves, crushed
½ tsp dried oregano

1   Heat oven to 220C/fan 200C/gas 7. Arrange the sausages in a roasting tin in a single layer and bake for 10 mins. Meanwhile, mix all the other ingredients with seasoning and 1 tbsp of water.

2   Pour the ketchup mixture over the sausages and mix well. Bake for 30 mins more, until the sausages are golden.

Per serving: 348 kcalories, protein 18g, carbohydrate 13g, fat 25g, saturated fat 8g, fibre none, sugar 6g, salt 1.78g

Healthy egg and chips

Treat the family to this easy twist on a fry up without the calories.

Serves 4 ■ prep 10 mins
■ cook 30 mins

500g/1lb 2oz potatoes, chopped
   into small chunks
2 shallots, chopped
1 tbsp olive oil
2 tsp dried oregano or 1 tsp fresh
   leaves
200g/8oz button mushrooms
4 eggs

1   Heat oven to 200C/fan 180C/gas 6. Tip the potatoes and shallots into a large, non-stick roasting tin, drizzle with the oil, sprinkle over the oregano, then mix everything together well. Bake for 15 mins, add the mushrooms, then cook for a further 10 mins until the potatoes are browned and tender.

2   Make four gaps in the vegetables and crack an egg into each space. Return to the oven for 3–4 mins or until the eggs are cooked to your liking, then divide among four plates.

Per serving: 218 kcalories, protein 11g, carbohydrate 22g, fat 10g, saturated fat 2g, fibre 2g, sugar 1g, salt 0.24g

Potato and Savoy cabbage soup with bacon ✳

Turn everyday ingredients into a warming soup.

Serves 4 ■ prep 10 mins ■ cook 10 mins

1 onion
1 carrot
1 celery stick
2 garlic cloves
1 tbsp olive oil, plus extra to serve
550g/1lb 4oz floury potatoes, peeled and cut into small cubes
1 litre/1¾ pints vegetable or chicken stock
8 rashers streaky bacon
¼ medium Savoy cabbage (about 200g/8oz)

1 Chop the onion, carrot, celery and garlic in a food processor. Heat the oil over a medium heat in a large pan. Add the vegetables and potatoes, season well, then reduce the heat and cover the pan. Gently cook for about 5 mins until starting to soften then add the stock, turn up the heat and bring to the boil. Simmer for 5 mins more, or until all the vegetables are tender.

2 While the soup is cooking, grill or fry the bacon until crisp, then cut into strips. Shred the cabbage, discarding the core.

3 Whizz the soup in the food processor until smooth, then return to the pan and add the cabbage. Simmer for a few mins until the cabbage is just tender, then season to taste and serve, scattered with the bacon.

Per serving: 336 kcalories, protein 21g, carbohydrate 32g, fat 15g, saturated fat 4g, fibre 5g, sugar 7g, salt 2.61g

Cauliflower cheese soup ✻

Soup and cauliflower cheese are classic comfort foods, and this is a perfect combination of the two. Great served in mugs for a TV supper.

1 Heat the butter in a large pan. Tip in the onion and cook until softened, about 5 mins, stirring often. Add the cauliflower, potato, stock and milk, and season with salt and pepper. Bring to the boil, then reduce the heat and leave to simmer for about 30 mins until the cauliflower is soft and the potato almost collapsing.

2 Whizz in a food processor or crush with a potato masher until you get a creamy, thick soup. Top up with more milk to thin a little, if serving in mugs. You can make ahead up to 2 days in advance, and cool, cover and leave in the fridge until needed or freeze for up to 1 month.

3 When ready to serve, warm through, ladle into mugs or bowls, then top with the cheese and stir through before eating.

Per serving: 188 kcalories, protein 13g, carbohydrate 13g, fat 10g, saturated fat 5g, fibre 3g, sugar 9g, salt 0.82g

Serves 6 ■ prep 10 mins ■ cook 35 mins

knob of butter
1 large onion, finely chopped
1 large cauliflower (about 900g/2lb), leaves trimmed and chopped into florets
1 potato, peeled and chopped into chunks
700ml/1¼ pints vegetable stock
400ml/14fl oz milk, plus extra to thin
100g/4oz mature cheddar, chopped into small chunks

Spiced carrot and lentil soup ✻

A hearty soup that can easily be served as a laid-back supper.

1 Heat a large pan and dry-fry the cumin seeds and chilli flakes for 1 min, or until they start to release their aromas. Scoop out half of the seeds with a spoon and set aside. Add the oil, carrot, lentils, stock and milk to the pan, and bring to the boil. Simmer for 15 mins until the lentils have swollen and softened.

2 Whizz the soup with a stick blender or in a food processor until smooth (or leave chunky, if you prefer). Season to taste and finish with a dollop of yogurt and a sprinkling of the reserved toasted spices. Serve with warmed naan breads.

Per serving: 238 kcalories, protein 11g, carbohydrate 34g, fat 7g, saturated fat 1g, fibre 5g, sugar none, salt 0.25g

TIP Soups are incredibly versatile, and you can play around with the spices. Substitute the chilli flakes and cumin seeds for a few teaspoons of harissa paste, if you have some in the cupboard. You could add cooked, shredded chicken at the end of cooking, too.

Serves 4 ■ prep 10 mins ■ cook 15 mins

2 tsp cumin seeds
pinch of dried chilli flakes
2 tbsp olive oil
600g/1lb 5oz carrots, washed and coarsely grated (no need to peel)
140g/5oz red split lentils
1 litre/1¾ pints hot vegetable stock
125ml/4fl oz milk

Asian-style chicken noodle soup

A simple soup that's ideal for using up leftover cooked chicken.

Serves 4 ■ prep 5 mins
■ cook 10 mins

140g/5oz stir-fry noodles
1.2 litres/2 pints chicken stock
2 kaffir lime leaves, shredded (or
   grated zest ½ lime)
small knob root ginger, grated
2 tbsp fresh coriander, finely
   chopped
410g can creamed-style sweetcorn
250g/9oz cooked chicken,
   shredded

1   Soak the stir-fry noodles for 4 mins in boiling water. Drain, rinse, and drain again. Divide among four soup bowls.

2   Heat the stock in a pan with the lime leaves, ginger and coriander. Bring to a boil and add the can of creamed-style corn and cooked, shredded chicken. Heat for 2 mins, and ladle over the noodles then serve.

Per serving: 374 kcalories, protein 32.2g, carbohydrate 45.5g, fat 8.4g, saturated fat 1.7g, fibre 2.6g, sugar 18.8, salt 3.25g

15-minute summer soup ❄

Barely wilting the watercress and mint gives this soup its vivid green colour and the most wonderful fresh, peppery flavour.

1   Heat the butter or oil in a pan, add the spring onions and courgettes and stir well. Cover and cook for 3 mins, then add the peas and stock, and return to the boil. Cover and simmer for a further 4 mins, then remove from the heat and stir in the watercress and mint until they are just wilted.

2   Purée in a food processor in two batches, adding yogurt to the second batch. Return to the pan, then add seasoning to taste. Serve hot or cold, drizzled with extra yogurt.

Per serving: 100 kcalories, protein 8g, carbohydrate 9g, fat 4g, saturated fat 2g, fibre 4g, sugar none, salt 0.81g

Serves 4 ■ prep 5–10 mins ■ cook 5 mins

knob of butter or splash of olive oil
bunch spring onions, chopped
3 courgettes, chopped
200g/8oz frozen peas
850ml/1½ pints vegetable stock
85g bag watercress, trimmed
large handful fresh mint leaves
2 rounded tbsp Greek yogurt, plus
   extra for drizzling

chapter 4

Freezer and storecupboard meals

There's a big difference between a well-stocked freezer or storecupboard and overloaded ones. If you open the door and they are bursting at the seams, but you still can't decide what to cook, then it's time for a clear-out. With the recipes in this chapter, an organized cupboard and a few essentials in the freezer, you will be able to cook up a meal in minutes.

The storecupboard and freezer are excellent aides to thrifty cooking. Using them wisely and stocking up on the right ingredients without over-filling will not only save you time in the shops but also considerably reduce your fresh-produce waste.

All the recipes in this chapter make the most of storecupboard or frozen ingredients to give you a selection of dinners. Some may require a few fresh ingredients too, but the main ingredients can be bought in advance and kept until needed — so you can reduce your shopping trips. Canned or frozen meat and vegetables, dried herbs, spices, pasta and bottled sauces are all cheaper than their fresh equivalents and add extra flavour to your meals with minimal effort — you just need to know how to make the best of them.

In this chapter we've also included a list of essential ingredients with a long shelf-life to keep in your cupboard as well as listing which fresh ingredients you can freeze and preserve safely. There are lots of raw and cooked ingredients that can be frozen providing they haven't been frozen before. This means if you end up with any leftovers, raw or cooked, you can freeze the excess.

Freezer and storecupboard know-how

As frozen and storecupboard ingredients last so much longer than fresh produce, it's easy to forget what you already have tucked away.

■ Check your freezer and cupboards before heading off to the shops, so that you don't accidently double up on anything.

■ Keep an eye on use-by dates, as even frozen and dried ingredients don't last for ever.

Top 10 storecupboard essentials

■ **Canned tomatoes**

Buy Italian chopped tomatoes if you can as their flavour is better.

■ **Pulses**

A great convenience food. Try lentils with sausages, butter beans to bulk out a stew, kidney beans for a quick chilli. Chickpeas are great mashed. Dried is economical, but canned are good for speed.

■ **Curry paste**

Find one that suits your chilli tolerance. Smear over meat before cooking; mix with mayonnaise or yogurt as a marinade.

■ **Honey**

Drizzle over a roast for an instant glaze. Add to dressings and sauces for sweetness and to cakes instead of some of the sugar.

■ **Mustard**

Adds a fiery hint to sauces, gravies and mash. Dijon and wholegrain are milder than English. Use the powder as a dry seasoning for beef, lamb or pork.

■ **Dried pasta**

There are so many different shapes to choose from. Keep a long pasta, such as spaghetti, and a chunkier shape, such as penne, to cover every occasion.

■ **Rice and grains**

Risotto and long grain rice are essential; basmati is nice to serve with spicy food. Couscous can be used in many ways and is incredibly quick and easy to prepare. Pearl barley is great for bulking up soups and stews.

■ **Soy sauce**

Use a Japanese variety, light or dark, to add extra flavour to any dish. Shake a little over raw meat or fish before grilling for an instant marinade.

■ **Stocks**

Vegetable bouillon powder can take the place of all the other stocks in recipes, and it is also delicious on its own as a warming broth.

■ Wine vinegar and oils

Balsamic and sherry vinegars are lovely, but red or white wine or cider vinegar are cheaper and more versatile – use them for cooking and in dressings. Distilled or malt vinegars are best shaken over chips or used for pickling onions. If you've got a vegetable oil or sunflower oil, an olive oil and extra-virgin olive oil, you've got it covered.

Not essential but useful

Anchovies, capers, coconut milk, dried mushrooms, noodles, nuts, olives and sundried tomatoes. Canned fish, such as tuna and mackerel can always be turned into a protein-rich lunch or supper. And a jar of pesto or tomato-based pasta sauce is just the thing for emergencies.

Freezing

There are plenty of foods you can keep in your freezer to preserve their shelf-life, and a few key ones you can't. Here are some examples:

Ingredients you can freeze

Cheese, mashed potato, milk, ham and sliced cooked meats, uncooked meats such as bacon and sausages, filled pasta, fruit (the texture of some soft fruits will go mushy when defrosted, so cook with them as it won't matter what they look like as much), vegetables (to preserve colour and texture, blanch first), meat, fish, fresh herbs (see tip for herb butter, page 154), bread (both whole loaves or rolls and breadcrumbs), pastry, crumble toppings or whole cooked crumbles, stocks or chicken carcasses (ready for making stock when you have time), soups, egg whites or yolks.

You should avoid freezing anything that contains cream or fromage frais. If you do, defrost the food slowly and heat gently. Cream and fromage frais will be affected by the thawing process and the texture will change.

Ingredients you can't freeze

Whole eggs, cooked rice, previously frozen cooked or raw ingredients in their same state.

Tortilla and bean salad

A classic Mediterranean salad with a bit of spice.

Serves 6 ▪ prep 10 mins ▪ cook 5 mins

1 tbsp vegetable oil
180g can sweetcorn, drained and rinsed
180g can kidney beans, drained and rinsed
225g bag mixed green leaves
handful plain tortilla chips
50ml/2fl oz soured cream
pinch of sugar
zest and juice ½ lime

1 Heat the oil in a frying pan and, when hot, stir in the sweetcorn. Cook for 3 mins, stirring often until the corn is browned, then remove and leave to cool.

2 Toss together the sweetcorn, kidney beans, salad leaves and tortilla chips. Mix the soured cream, sugar and lime zest and juice for the dressing. Drizzle over the salad and serve.

Per serving: 109 kcalories, protein 3g, carbohydrate 14g, fat 5g, saturated fat 1g, fibre 2g, sugar 2g, salt 0.46g

Homemade houmous with pitta chips

Over the years houmous seems to have become a kids' staple. It's really simple to make, costs very little, and you can be sure it's low in salt (some bought types are full of it).

Serves 4 as a light lunch or supper ▪ prep 10 mins ▪ cook 10 mins

3 pitta breads
5 tbsp olive oil
410g can chickpeas, rinsed and drained
½ tsp ground cumin
1 garlic clove, crushed
juice 1 lemon

1 Heat oven to 180C/fan 160C/gas 4. Cut each pitta in half so it separates into two really thin slices, then cut into strips or wedges. Lightly grease a shallow baking sheet with a little of the olive oil and arrange the pitta slices on top. Cook in the oven for 10 mins until crisp, then leave to cool. They can be stored in an airtight container for 4–5 days.

2 To make the houmous, tip the chickpeas into a food processor. Add all the remaining ingredients and 3 tbsp of cold water and blend together. Keep adding water, a tbsp at a time, until you get a smooth, spoonable paste. Tip into a bowl and serve. The houmous can be kept in the fridge for up to 3 days.

Per serving: 227 kcalories, protein 7g, carbohydrate 28g, fat 11g, saturated fat 1g, fibre 3g, sugar 1g, salt 0.64g

Spicy tomato baked eggs ❄

Vary this dish by flavouring the simple tomato sauce with whatever you have to hand – curry powder, pesto or fresh herbs.

1 Heat the oil in a frying pan with a lid, then soften the onions, chilli, garlic and coriander stalks for 5 mins until soft. Stir in the tomatoes and sugar, then bubble for 8–10 mins until thick. The tomato mix can be frozen at this stage for 1 month.

2 Using the back of a large spoon, make 4 dips in the sauce, then crack an egg into each one. Put the lid on the pan, then cook over a low heat for 6–8 mins, until the eggs are done to your liking. Scatter with the coriander leaves and serve with crusty bread.

Per serving: 340 kcalories, protein 21g, carbohydrate 21g, fat 20g, saturated fat 5g, fibre 6g, sugar 17g, salt 1.25g

Serves 2 ▪ prep 5 mins
▪ cook about 20 mins

1 tbsp olive oil
2 red onions, chopped
1 red chilli, deseeded and finely
   chopped
1 garlic clove, chopped
small bunch fresh coriander, stalks
   and leaves chopped separately
2 × 400g cans cherry tomatoes
1 tsp caster sugar
4 eggs

Tuna and chickpea patties

Using canned chickpeas instead of potatoes means these spicy bites are really quick to make.

1 Mix the yogurt with half the coriander in a small bowl. Cover and chill until needed.

2 Tip the chickpeas into a food processor. Blitz for just a few secs so they keep some of their texture. Transfer to a large bowl. Flake in the tuna and mix in the onion, garlic, lemon juice, cumin, chilli and the rest of the coriander. Season, then gently stir to mix all the ingredients. Shape into 12 patties with your hands. Dust with flour.

3 Heat half the oil in a large frying pan. Cook six patties for 5–6 mins, turning over after 3 mins. Cook the rest and keep warm.

4 Put the tomatoes in the pan. Cook over a high heat for 30–40 secs until warmed through and starting to soften. Serve with the patties (three per person) and the coriander dip.

Per serving: 327 kcalories, protein 33g, carbohydrate 32g, fat 8g, saturated fat 1g, fibre 6g, sugar none, salt 1.51g

Serves 4 ▪ prep 15 mins
▪ cook 25 mins

150g pot low-fat natural yogurt
good handful fresh coriander,
   roughly chopped
2 × 410g cans chickpeas, drained
   and rinsed
400g can tuna in brine, drained
1 small onion, finely chopped
1 garlic clove, crushed
2 tbsp fresh lemon juice
1 tsp cumin seeds
½ tsp crushed dried chillies
2 tbsp plain flour
4 tsp vegetable oil
12 cherry tomatoes, halved

Tuna melt potato wedges

This is perfect for those days when you come home with a hungry family and have nothing prepared to feed them. A real life-saver – serve with some veg from the freezer.

Serves 4 ■ prep 10 mins ■ cook 20–25 mins

750g pack frozen potato wedges
4 tbsp mayonnaise
1 shallot or ½ small onion, very finely chopped
100g/4oz cheddar, grated
2 × 200g cans tuna in spring water, drained
bunch fresh parsley, chopped (optional)

1 Heat oven to 220C/fan 200C/gas 7. Tip the potato wedges on to a large baking sheet in a single layer. Bake for 10 mins. Meanwhile, mix together the mayonnaise, shallot or onion, cheese, tuna and parsley.

2 Tip the potato wedges into a large ovenproof serving dish and spoon over the tuna mixture. Pop back in the oven for a further 12 mins, until bubbling, then serve.

Per serving: 487 kcalories, protein 25g, carbohydrate 35g, fat 28g, saturated fat 11g, fibre 3g, sugar 1g, salt 3.15g

Easy oven frittata

This is such a versatile recipe. You can vary the fillings depending on what you have in the fridge.

Serves 4 ■ prep 20 mins ■ cook 40 mins

½ tsp olive oil
85g/3oz fusilli or macaroni
1 leek or 1 bunch spring onions, chopped
85g/3oz frozen or canned sweetcorn
85g/3oz frozen peas
1 red pepper, deseeded and chopped
2 eggs
150ml/¼ pint milk
1 tbsp fresh thyme leaves
50g/2oz extra mature cheddar, grated
2 tbsp finely grated parmesan

1 Heat oven to 190C/fan 170C/gas 5. Grease a 1.2 litre baking dish with the olive oil.

2 Cook the pasta in salted boiling water in a large pan for 8 mins. Add all the vegetables and cook for another 2–3 mins until the pasta is tender and the vegetables slightly softened. Drain, then tip into the baking dish and mix well.

3 Beat the eggs and milk in a jug and add the thyme. Mix the two cheeses together and add most of them to the egg mixture, then season. Pour into the baking dish, stir gently, then scatter the rest of the cheese on top. Bake for 35–40 mins until set and golden. Cool for a few mins, then serve with a green salad.

Per serving: 268 kcalories, protein 14.9g, carbohydrate 28.9g, fat 11.1g, saturated fat 5g, fibre 3.3g, sugar 7.7g, salt 0.61g

Storecupboard corn pancakes

You can use fresh, frozen or canned sweetcorn for this great brunch recipe or replace the bacon with field mushrooms for a satisfying veggie dish.

1 If using fresh corn, remove the husk and slice the kernels from the cob with a large sharp knife, then cook them in a pan of boiling water for 5 mins. Drain and leave to cool.

2 Whisk together the eggs, milk and butter. Whisk in the flour and a large pinch of salt until smooth, then mix in the corn and the spring onions. Set aside.

3 Heat the grill to high. Put the tomatoes cut-side up on a large baking tray, drizzle with olive oil and season with salt and pepper. Lay the bacon next to the tomatoes in a single layer on the tray. Grill for 8–10 mins until the tomatoes have softened and the bacon is crispy, turning the rashers over half-way through.

4 While the bacon's crisping up, heat the sunflower oil in a large frying pan. Add 4 large spoonfuls of the batter and fry for 1–2 mins on each side until the pancakes are puffed up and golden. Lift out on to a plate lined with kitchen paper, then repeat to make four more pancakes. Bring to the table with a bottle of chilli sauce.

Per serving: 309 kcalories, protein 7g, carbohydrate 26g, fat 20g, saturated fat 6g, fibre 2g, added sugar none, salt 0.43g

Serves 4 ■ prep 15–20 mins ■ cook 15–20 mins

1 fresh cob, husks removed, or
   330g can sweetcorn, drained
2 eggs
5 tbsp milk
25g/1oz butter, melted
85g/3oz self-raising flour
2 spring onions, finely chopped
4 tomatoes, halved
olive oil, for drizzling
8 rashers good-quality bacon
4 tbsp sunflower oil, for shallow
   frying

Scrambled egg muffin

If you have eggs in your fridge, you can always make a meal. If you don't have muffins, any toasted bread will do.

1 Melt the butter in a pan, then tip in the beaten eggs and scramble. When almost done, stir in the chopped tomatoes and the basil leaves.

2 Toast the muffins and when the egg is ready, pile it on top and serve.

Per serving: 399 kcalories, protein 24.4g, carbohydrate 36.5g, fat 18.3g, saturated fat 6g, fibre 2.7g, sugar 3.7g, salt 2.74g

Serves 2 ■ prep 5 mins ■ cook 5–10 mins

knob of buttter
4 eggs, beaten
handful sundried tomatoes,
   chopped
handful fresh basil leaves, torn
2 English muffins

Corned beef hash

You could offer a choice of tomato ketchup, brown sauce, Worcestershire sauce or Tabasco to serve with the hash.

Serves 4 ▪ prep 20–30 mins ▪ cook 35 mins

4 large potatoes (about 900g–1kg/2–2¼lb), chopped into 2cm squares
340g can corned beef
1 large onion, roughly chopped
knob of butter
4 tbsp vegetable oil

1   Put the potatoes into a pan of boiling water, add a good pinch of salt, cover and bring back to the boil for 2–3 mins until just tender.

2   Meanwhile, cut the corned beef into chunks that are roughly the same size as the potatoes. When the potatoes are tender, drain well.

3   Put the butter and 2 tbsp of the oil into a large non-stick frying pan. Heat until the butter is foaming. Tip in the onion, stir well and cook for about 5 mins until the onion becomes tinged golden brown. Pour in the remaining oil and increase the heat slightly.

4   Tip in the potatoes and corned beef, then sprinkle in a pinch of salt and a good grinding of black pepper. Stir to mix everything together then cook for 15 mins, folding and turning the hash every 2–3 mins, until it starts to turn golden brown. You need to leave the potatoes undisturbed long enough to crisp underneath, but not so long that they burn.

5   Reduce the heat and continue to cook for another 5 mins, folding and turning the hash every so often to fry everything evenly. Check the seasoning then serve straight from the pan.

Per serving: 487 kcalories, protein 28g, carbohydrate 42g, fat 24g, saturated fat 7g, fibre 4g, added sugar none, salt 2.14g

You can cook lots of variation on the basic Corned beef hash.
Here are some of our favourite ideas:

Baked bean hash

Tip a 200g can of baked beans into the hash after the 5 mins
cooking in step 5, then stir for 2 mins until the beans are hot.
This makes a good vegetarian hash if you omit the corned beef.

Hash with eggs

After the 5 mins cooking in step 5, make four nests in the hash with
the back of a metal spoon. Crack an egg into each. Cover the pan
with a lid or foil, turn the heat down to medium and cook for 5–7
mins until the eggs are set.

Red 'flannel' hash

Chop 4 small cooked beetroot into quite small. After the 5 mins
cooking time in step 5, add the beetroot to the hash, stir to mix
and cook for 2 mins until hot.

Cheesy hash

Cook the hash in a flameproof and ovenproof pan. About
10 minutes before it's cooked, grate 100g cheddar and sprinkle
it over the top. Heat the grill to high and pop the hash under
the grill for 5 mins until golden and bubbling.

Pizza Margherita

If you've never made pizza from scratch then try this — it tastes so much better than any bought version and isn't difficult to do.

Serves 4 (makes 2 pizzas)
■ **prep 25 mins** ■ **cook 10 mins**

for the base
300g/10oz strong bread flour
1 tsp instant yeast (from a sachet or tub)
1 tsp salt
1 tbsp olive oil, plus extra for drizzling

for the tomato sauce
100ml/3fl oz passata
handful fresh basil or 1 tsp dried
1 garlic clove, crushed

for the topping
125g ball mozzarella, sliced
handful grated or shaved parmesan
handful cherry tomatoes, halved
handful fresh basil leaves (optional), scattered over to serve

1 To make the base, put the flour into a large bowl, then stir in the yeast and salt. Make a well, pour in 200ml of warm water and the olive oil, and bring together with a wooden spoon until you have a soft, fairly wet dough. Turn on to a lightly floured surface and knead for 5 mins until smooth. Cover with a tea towel and set aside. You can leave the dough to rise if you like, but it's not essential for a thin crust.

2 To make the sauce, mix together the passata, basil and garlic, then season to taste. Leave to stand at room temperature while you get on with shaping the base.

3 If you've let the dough rise, give it a quick knead. Split the dough into two balls. On a floured surface, roll out each dough ball into large rounds, about 25cm across, using a rolling pin. The dough needs to be very thin as it will rise in the oven. Lift the rounds on to two floured baking sheets.

4 Heat oven to 240C/fan 220C/gas 9. Put another baking sheet in the oven on the top shelf. Smooth sauce over each base with the back of a spoon. Scatter with the cheeses and the tomatoes, drizzle with olive oil and season. Put one pizza, still on its baking sheet, on top of the preheated sheet. Bake for 8–10 mins until crisp. Serve with a little more olive oil, black pepper and basil leaves, if using. Repeat step 4 with the remaining pizza.

Per serving: 431 kcalories, protein 19g, carbohydrate 59g, fat 15g, saturated fat 7g, fibre 3g, sugar 2g, salt 1.87g

TIP One of the best things about making pizzas is choosing the toppings. Just don't overload the base or it won't cook through in time. Try these ideas, or do half and half:
■ olives, ham and chargrilled artichokes
■ spicy sausage, chilli or jalapeños and sliced tomato
■ spinach, garlic, gorgonzola cheese and a whole egg cracked on top
■ creamy mascarpone, pesto, roasted red peppers and sliced mushrooms

Red onion, feta and olive tart

A spin on the popular pastry tart. You can vary the toppings to use whatever you have in the cupboard – sundried tomatoes, pesto and ham all work well.

Serve 4 ▪ prep 10 mins
▪ cook 15–20 mins

2 tbsp olive oil
2 large red onions, chopped into
    thin wedges
2 tbsp light muscovado sugar
2 tbsp balsamic vinegar
375g sheet ready-rolled puff pastry
100g/4oz feta, crumbled
175g/6oz black olives, pitted and
    chopped
1 tbsp olive oil

1   Heat oven to 220C/fan 200C/gas 7. Heat the oil in a frying pan, then gently fry the onions for about 10 mins until golden and soft. Add the sugar and balsamic vinegar, then cook for a further 5 mins until the juices are reduced and syrupy. Leave to cool.

2   Unroll the puff pastry on a baking sheet. Score a line a finger-width in from the edge all the way around, then cover the middle with the onion mix. Scatter over the feta and olives. Season and drizzle the olive oil over the topping.

3   Bake for 15 mins or until the pastry is risen and golden and the base is crisp. Cut into squares and serve with a green salad.

Per serving: 619 kcalories, protein 11g, carbohydrate 51g, fat 43g, saturated fat 14g, fibre 3g, sugar 15g, salt 2.33g

Mozzarella, ham and pesto pizzas

Create this speedy pizza using a clever ready-made base idea.

1 Heat the grill to high, put the pittas on the grill rack and heat for about 1 min while you slice the mozzarella into five pieces.

2 Turn the pittas over and spread each one with 1 tsp of pesto, then top with a mozzarella slice. Pile the ham on top, so it looks quite ruffled, then tear the final mozzarella slice into four, put it on top of the ham and grind over some black pepper. Return to the grill for 3–4 mins more until melted and starting to turn golden.

Per serving: 491 kcalories, protein 36g, carbohydrate 41g, fat 21g, saturated fat 12g, fibre 1.6g, added sugar none, salt 3.34g

Serves 2 ▪ prep 5 mins ▪ cook 5 mins

4 mini pitta breads
150g ball mozzarella
4 tsp pesto
85g/3oz smoked wafer-thin ham
   or Prosciutto

DIY kofta burgers ✳

A quick, easy and cheap variation on a burger.

Serves 4 ▪ prep 30 mins
▪ cook 20 mins

500g/1lb 2oz lamb mince
1 onion, finely chopped
½ garlic bulb, broken into cloves
  and finely chopped
3 tbsp garam masala
big handful fresh coriander,
  chopped (optional)
½ tbsp chilli sauce, plus extra to
  serve
to serve
4 pitta breads
2 tomatoes, halved and sliced
½ small red cabbage, shredded
½ red onion, finely chopped
  (optional)
150g pot natural yogurt

1 Tip all the burger ingredients into a large bowl with a good pinch of salt. Mix everything together using clean hands. Pat the mix into 16 small burgers. These can now be frozen for up to 1 month or chilled up to a day ahead.

2 To cook, heat the grill to its high and lay the burgers in a single layer on a baking sheet (you may need to do this in batches, depending on how big your sheet is). Grill on the highest shelf for 5–6 mins on each side until browned and cooked through. Pile the burgers on to a platter and serve with all the accompaniments, so everyone can construct their own sandwich.

Per serving: 295 kcalories, protein 26g, carbohydrate 8g, fat 18g, saturated fat 8g, fibre none, sugar 2g, salt 0.37g

Fragrant lamb flatbreads

A healthy alternative to pizza.

1 Heat oven to 220C/fan 200C/gas 7. Make the bread mix following the pack instructions. Divide into two and roll out into large ovals, then transfer them to a large, floured baking sheet.

2 In a bowl, combine the onion, lamb, garlic, spices and yogurt, and season. Crumble over the dough almost to the edges, then scatter over the pine nuts. Bake for 15–18 mins until the bread is golden and crisp and the meat is browned. Sprinkle over the mint, then serve with a green salad.

Per serving: 377 kcalories, protein 22g, carbohydrate 47g, fat 12g, saturated fat 4g, fibre 3g, sugar 3g, salt 1.24g

TO MAKE YOUR OWN DOUGH
250g/9oz strong white flour
½ tsp salt
1 tsp sugar
1 tsp easy blend yeast from a 7g sachet
150ml/¼ pint warm water
Mix together the flour, salt, sugar and yeast. Add the water and mix to a soft dough. Knead for 2 mins on a lightly floured surface, then roll out. Add the topping as above. Leave in a warm place to rise for 15 mins before serving.

Serves 4 ■ prep 10 mins ■ cook 18 mins

½ x 500g pack bread mix – or make your own
1 onion, finely chopped
250g/9oz lean minced lamb
1 garlic clove, crushed
1 tsp ground cumin
1 tsp ground coriander
2 tbsp natural yogurt
2 tbsp pine nuts
handful fresh mint, chopped (or use a sprinkling of dried)

Pepper-prawn skewers

Keep a bag of prawns in the freezer to whip this up at a moment's notice. This dish is really good on the barbecue too.

1 Pat the prawns dry on kitchen paper. Pureé the chilli, pepper, oil, zest and a pinch of salt. Fold gently into the prawns, then leave to marinate in the fridge for at least 20 mins.

2 Heat a griddle until hot. Divide the prawns between the skewers. Griddle for 3 mins on each side, brushing with excess marinade. Serve with a green salad and plenty of crusty bread.

Per serving: 203 kcalories, protein 18g, carbohydrate 1g, fat 14g, saturated fat 2g, fibre 1g, added sugar none, salt 0.77g

Serves 4 ■ prep 10 mins, plus marinating ■ cook 10 mins

400g bag frozen raw peeled tiger prawns, defrosted
1 large red chilli, roughly chopped
1 ready roasted red pepper, deseeded and chopped
4 tbsp olive oil
zest 1 lemon
4 long or 8 short skewers (soaked for 30 mins if wooden)

Meatballs with pesto mash

A rustic Italian-style family dinner with herby mashed potatoes.

1 Mix the mince with half the chopped basil, the Worcestershire sauce and some seasoning to taste, then use your hands to shape into 16 meatballs. Heat a non-stick frying pan, add the oil, then fry the meatballs, turning, for 5 mins until browned. Tip in the passata and the remaining chopped basil. Simmer gently for 10 mins until the meatballs are cooked through.

2 Meanwhile, boil the potatoes for 10–15 mins until tender. Drain well, then return to the pan over a low heat and mash (leaving the heat on will help to dry out the potatoes for a fluffier mash). Stir in the milk, then marble through the pesto. Pile the mash on to four plates, spoon over the meatballs and serve scattered with the reserved basil leaves.

Per serving: 488 kcalories, protein 28.8g, carbohydrate 50.8g, fat 20.3g, saturated fat 8.6g, fibre 3.5g, sugar 6.7g, salt 0.94g

Serves 4 ■ prep 15 mins ■ cook 15 mins

400g/14oz minced beef
small bunch fresh basil leaves, roughly chopped, reserving a few whole, to serve
1 tbsp Worcestershire sauce
1 tsp olive oil
½ x 700g bottle passata with onions and garlic
1kg/2lb 4oz potatoes, peeled and chopped
150ml/¼ pint milk
2 tbsp basil pesto

One-pan summer chicken

Get your carb fix from the butter beans in this simple supper.

Serves 2 ■ prep 5 mins
■ cook 35 mins

2 red peppers
large handful fresh basil leaves
1 garlic clove, chopped
2 plum tomatoes, halved
2 chicken leg quarters, skin on
2 tbsp olive oil
410g can butter beans, drained
   and rinsed

1   Heat oven to 220C/fan 200C/gas 7. Cut the peppers in half lengthways and scoop out the seeds and white membrane, but try to keep the stalk attached. Stuff each pepper half with basil (but don't use it all), the garlic and a tomato half.

2   Snuggle the stuffed pepper halves alongside the chicken in a roasting tin. Drizzle the oil over everything and season with pepper and salt, if using. Roast the chicken and the peppers for 25–30 mins until the chicken is golden with a crisp skin, and the peppers and tomatoes have softened and wrinkled. Lift the chicken and the stuffed peppers on to a plate, tipping the peppers so that the tasty juices drain into the roasting tin.

3   Put the tin over a low flame and pour in a splash of water. Add the beans and stir well to release any sticky bits from the roasting tin. Stir the remaining basil through the beans and serve them alongside the chicken and peppers.

Per serving: 618 kcalories, protein 41.6g, carbohydrate 28.4g, fat 38.3g, saturated fat 10.1g, fibre 8.8g, sugar 13.3g, salt 1.73g

Toad-in-the-hole with red onions and thyme batter

We bought low-fat sausages and used skimmed milk, but you can use whatever you have to hand.

Serves 4 ▪ prep 30–40 mins ▪ cook 40 mins

1 red onion, chopped into wedges, layers separated
8 thick pork sausages
1 tsp olive oil
for the batter
100g/4oz plain flour
1 medium egg
300ml/½ pint milk
2 tsp wholegrain mustard
1 tsp fresh thyme leaves

1 Heat oven to 200C/fan 180C/gas 6. Tip the onions into a small shallow non-stick roasting tin (about 23x30cm). Arrange the sausages on top of the onions, then add the oil and roast for 20 mins.

2 While they are cooking, make the batter. Sift the flour into a bowl, crack the egg into the centre and beat in the milk a little at a time to make a smooth batter. Stir in the mustard and thyme, and season with salt and pepper.

3 Take the sausage tin out of the over and quickly pour over the batter. Return to the oven for 40 mins until the batter is risen and golden and the sausages are cooked.

Per serving (using low-fat sausages and skimmed milk):
293 kcalories, protein 23g, carbohydrate 36g, fat 7g, saturated fat 2g, fibre 1g, sugar none, salt 2.36g

Leek, butter bean and chorizo gratin

Leftover chorizo makes a spicy Spanish-style supper.

Serves 4 ■ prep 10 mins ■ cook 25 mins

1 tbsp olive oil
85g/3oz chorizo sausage, roughly chopped
4 large leeks, finely chopped
3 garlic cloves, chopped
100ml/3½fl oz dry sherry
2 × 410g cans butter beans, drained and rinsed
500ml/18fl oz vegetable stock
85g/3oz bread, torn into pieces

1 Heat oven to 200C/fan 180C/gas 6. Heat the oil in a pan and fry the chorizo for a few mins until slightly crisp. Remove the chorizo using a slotted spoon, leaving the oil in the pan. Add the leeks and half the garlic to the pan and cook for 5 mins in the chorizo oil until soft. Pour in the sherry, beans and stock. Season, then bubble for 5 mins.

2 Meanwhile, blitz the bread to coarse crumbs with the remaining garlic. Tip the leek mixture into an ovenproof dish, stir in the chorizo and scatter over the crumbs. Bake for 10 mins until golden, then serve with crusty bread.

Per serving: 275 kcalories, protein 15g, carbohydrate 32g, fat 9g, saturated fat 2g, fibre 9g, sugar 7g, salt 2.41g

Mixed bean goulash ❄

Serve with soured cream and toasted ciabatta slices, or a mound of steamed rice.

Serves 2 ■ prep 5 mins ■ cook 20 mins

2 tbsp olive oil
1 large onion, finely chopped
1 garlic clove, crushed
1 tbsp smoked paprika
400g can chopped tomatoes
410g can mixed beans, drained and rinsed

1 Heat the oil in a large pan, then fry the onion for 5 mins until beginning to soften. Add the garlic and paprika, and cook for 1 min, then stir in the tomatoes and half a can of water. Simmer gently for 10 mins until the sauce has thickened.

2 Tip in the mixed beans and continue to cook for a further 2 mins to heat them through. When ready, spoon the goulash into warm bowls and serve.

Per serving: 460 kcalories, protein 17g, carbohydrate 39g, fat 28g, saturated fat 11g, fibre 11g, sugar 15g, salt 1.68g

10-minute tortellini

Some ready meals, like this filled pasta, can be turned into a great instant supper.

Serves 2 ▪ prep 5 mins
▪ cook 5 mins

250g pack fresh spinach and
 ricotta tortellini
1 tbsp olive oil
250g pack cherry tomatoes
40g fresh parsley leaves, roughly
 chopped
3 tbsp grated parmesan

1   Boil the pasta for 2 mins until just cooked. Meanwhile, heat the oil in a frying pan and sizzle the tomatoes until they start to blister.

2   When the pasta is cooked, drain it quickly, reserving some cooking water. Put the tomatoes back on a high heat. Tip in the pasta, parsley, a splash of cooking water and most of the parmesan. Bubble everything together, season to taste and serve with the remaining parmesan.

Per serving: 482 kcalories, protein 18g, carbohydrate 62g, fat 20g, saturated fat 8g, fibre 4g, added sugar none, salt 1.5g

Best-ever macaroni cheese ❄

A filling, economical family supper that you could also serve for a casual meal with friends. We used full-fat milk to make it extra creamy.

1 Heat oven to 200C/fan 180C/gas 6. Spread the diced bread over a baking sheet, drizzle with the melted butter and some seasoning. Bake for 6 mins until crisp and set aside.

2 Boil the pasta for 2 mins less than it says on the pack. Meanwhile, melt the remaining butter in a pan. Add the garlic and mustard, cook for 1 min then stir in the flour. Cook for 1 min more then gradually whisk in the milk until you have a lump-free sauce. Simmer for 5 mins, whisking constantly until thickened. Take off the heat then stir in all the cheddar and half the parmesan. Stir in the pasta and some seasoning, and tip into a large ovenproof dish. Scatter over the bread and remaining parmesan, then bake for 20 mins until golden.

Per serving: 837 kcalories, protein 37.9g, carbohydrate 88.7g, fat 39.2g, saturated fat 23.4g, fibre 3.4g, sugar 8.8g, salt 1.92g

Serves 4 ■ prep 10 mins ■ cook 40 mins

50g/2oz fresh baguette, sliced into small chunks
2 tbsp butter, plus 1 tbsp melted butter
350g/12oz pasta
1 garlic clove, finely chopped
1 tsp English mustard powder
3 tbsp plain flour
500ml/18fl oz milk
250g/9oz mature cheddar, grated
50g/2oz parmesan, grated

Creamy pea and chive barley risotto

Pearl barley cooks in a similar way to risotto rice and gives a deliciously creamy and filling bowlful.

1 Heat the oil in a large, deep pan, then gently fry the onion for 3–4 mins. Stir in the pearl barley, sizzle for a few mins, then pour in about a third of the stock. Simmer for 20 mins, stirring occasionally, adding more stock gradually as it is absorbed. After 15 mins, stir in the peas. When the risotto is ready there should be some liquid left and the barley should be cooked through.

2 Turn off the heat and let the risotto sit for a minute, then stir in the cream cheese and most of the chives. Season well and serve with the rest of the chives scattered over the top.

Per serving: 656 kcalories, protein 20g, carbohydrate 104g, fat 20g, saturated fat 6g, fibre 8g, sugar 12g, salt 1.41g

Serves 2 ■ prep 5 mins ■ cook 25 mins

2 tbsp olive oil
1 onion, finely chopped
200g/8oz pearl barley
1.2 litres/2 pints vegetable stock
140g/5oz frozen peas
100g/4oz light soft cheese with chives
small bunch fresh chives, snipped

Sweet potato and pineapple korma

A mild curry made with a few ingredients and minimum hassle.

1 In a pan, toss the korma paste with the sweet potato, then pour in the coconut milk and half a can of water. Cook for about 15mins or until the sweet potato is tender.

2 Tip in the pineapple chunks, simmer for 2 mins to heat them through, then season to taste. Scatter with the coriander and serve with naan bread.

Per serving: 617 kcalories, protein 6.7g, carbohydrate 70.7g, fat 36.2g, saturated fat 28.5g, fibre 5.7g, sugar 38.8g, salt 1.35g

Serves 2 ■ prep 5 mins ■ cook 20 mins

2 tbsp korma paste
2 sweet potatoes, peeled and chopped into large chunks
400g can coconut milk
400g can pineapple chunks, drained
handful fresh coriander leaves, chopped

Broad bean pilaf

Broad beans make a change from peas, and as the British season is so short, they're an ideal veg to keep in the freezer.

Serves 4 ▪ prep 30 mins, plus soaking ▪ cook 15 mins

200g/8oz basmati rice
300g/10oz frozen broad beans, defrosted and podded (see tip below)
50g/2oz butter
4 spring onions, finely chopped
handful pine nuts
½ tsp ground allspice
bunch fresh dill, fronds removed and roughly chopped

TIP Once podded, broad beans come with a tough outside coat. If you have time, slip the sweet little beans out of their shells after they have been blanched and cooled.

1 Wash the rice in several changes of cold water until the water runs clear, then soak it in warm water with a pinch of salt for 30 mins. Meanwhile, cook the broad beans in boiling unsalted water for just 2 mins. Drain the beans, then tip into ice-cold water and leave to cool.

2 Heat the butter in a pan, then fry the spring onions, pine nuts, allspice and half the dill for a few mins until the pine nuts are toasted. Drain the rice and add to the pan, stirring to coat in the butter. Cover the rice with about 1cm of water, then put a lid on the pan and bring to the boil. Stir once, then reduce the heat to low, cover again and leave for 5 mins. Turn off the heat and leave the rice undisturbed for 10 mins. Finally, stir the beans through the rice, pile on to a serving platter, scraping any golden crispy bits from the pan, and scatter with the remaining dill.

Per serving: 351 kcalories, protein 9g, carbohydrate 46g, fat 16g, saturated fat 7g, fibre 5g, sugar 2g, salt 0.20g

Ham, artichoke and lemon pilaf

Whip up this filling one-pot dish in minutes.

Serves 4 ▪ prep 5 mins ▪ cook 15 mins

1 tbsp olive oil
1 onion, chopped
250g/9oz basmati rice
700ml/1¼ pints vegetable stock
300g/10oz artichoke hearts, from a jar, chopped
300g/10oz sliced ham, chopped
zest and juice 2 lemons
3 tbsp fresh mint, chopped

1 Heat the oil in a large pan, then add the onion and fry for a couple of mins until starting to soften. Stir in the rice, then pour in the stock and bring to the boil. Cover and cook for 5 mins.

2 Add the artichokes, ham, half the lemon zest and all of the juice to the pan. Cover and cook for 5–7 mins more until the rice is tender. Stir in the mint, then divide among four bowls and scatter over the remaining zest.

Per serving: 509 kcalories, protein 22g, carbohydrate 57g, fat 23g, saturated fat 4g, fibre 3g, sugar 4g, salt 3.66g

Easy risotto with bacon and peas

Creamy peas and rice are complemented by the crispy saltiness of the bacon.

1 Finely chop the onion. Heat the olive oil and butter in a pan, then add the onion and fry for about 7 mins until lightly browned. Add the bacon and fry for a further 5 mins, until crisp.

2 Add the rice and stock, and bring to the boil. Stir well, then reduce the heat and cook, covered, for 15–20 mins until the rice is almost tender.

3 Stir in the peas, season with a little salt and pepper, and heat for a further 3 mins, until the peas are cooked. Serve sprinkled with freshly grated parmesan and freshly ground black pepper.

Per serving: 396 kcalories, protein 14g, carbohydrate 64g, fat 11g, saturated fat 4g, fibre 3g, sugar none, salt 1.88g

■ **Serves 4** ■ **prep 10 mins** ■ **cook 35–40 mins**

1 onion
2 tbsp olive oil
knob of butter
6 rashers streaky bacon, chopped
300g/10oz risotto rice
1 litre/1¾ pints hot vegetable stock
100g/4oz frozen peas
grated parmesan, to serve

Crab and lemon spaghetti

With minimum shopping, you can serve a light and summery pasta dish in less than half an hour.

1 Cook the spaghetti according to the pack instructions, stirring a couple of times to stop it sticking.

2 Tip the crabmeat into a sieve. Drain well. Heat 2 tbsp of the oil in a large frying pan, add the garlic and chilli, and fry for 1 min. Tip the crabmeat into the pan with the wine and a squeeze of lemon juice, season with salt and pepper and heat through for a min or so, stirring constantly.

3 Drain the pasta, return it to the pan and tip in the crab mixture, the last tbsp of oil and the parsley. Toss everything together and serve.

Per serving: 410 kcalories, protein 16.1g, carbohydrate 65.3g, fat 10g, saturated fat 1.4g, fibre 2.8g, sugar 3.2g, salt 0.42g

Serves 4 ■ prep 5 mins ■ cook 10–15 mins

350g/12oz spaghetti or linguine
170g can crabmeat
3 tbsp olive oil
1 garlic clove, finely chopped
1 red chilli, deseeded and finely chopped
½ glass white wine
squeeze fresh lemon juice
20g pack fresh parsley, roughly chopped

Hearty pasta soup

This meal in a bowl is a storecupboard winner.

Serves 4 ■ prep 5 mins
■ cook 25 mins

1 tbsp olive oil
2 carrots, chopped
1 large onion, finely chopped
1 litre/1¾ pints vegetable stock
400g can chopped tomatoes with
    garlic
200g/8oz frozen mixed peas and
    beans
250g pack fresh filled pasta (we
    used tortellini with ricotta and
    spinach)
handful fresh basil leaves,
    chopped (optional)
grated parmesan, to serve

1 Heat the oil in a pan. Fry the carrots and onion for 5 mins until starting to soften. Add the stock and tomatoes, then simmer for 10 mins. After 5 mins, add the peas and beans.

2 Once the veg is tender, stir in the pasta. Return to the boil and simmer for 2 mins until the pasta is just cooked. Stir in the basil, if using. Season, then serve in bowls topped with a sprinkling of parmesan.

Per serving: 286 kcalories, protein 11g, carbohydrate 44g, fat 9g, saturated fat 3g, fibre 6g, sugar 11g, salt 0.88g

Versatile veg soup ❋

A handy soup to make before your shopping day, to use up odd leftovers of fresh veg.

Serves 2 ■ prep 10 mins
■ cook 10–15 mins

200g/8oz raw vegetables, such
    as onions, celery and carrots,
    chopped
300g/10oz potatoes, peeled and
    chopped into cubes
700ml/1¼ pints vegetable stock

1 Fry the chopped raw vegetables with the potatoes in a little oil for a few mins until beginning to soften. Cover with the stock and simmer for 10–15 mins until the veg is tender.

2 Blend until smooth, then season. Will freeze for up to 1 month. Serve with a dollop of crème fraîche and some fresh herbs if you have them.

Per serving: 159 kcalories, protein 5.3g, carbohydrate 34.5g, fat 0.9g, saturated fat 0.1g, fibre 5.3g, sugar 8g, salt 0.55g

Moroccan chickpea soup ❄

Something different for vegetarians. This is a good recipe to make double quantities of and freeze a batch.

1   Heat the oil in a large pan, then fry the onion and celery gently for 10 mins until softened, stirring frequently. Tip in the cumin and fry for another min.

2   Turn up the heat, then add the stock, tomatoes and chickpeas, plus a good grind of black pepper. Simmer for 8 mins. Throw in the broad beans and lemon juice, cook for a further 2 mins. Season to taste, then top with a sprinkling of lemon zest and the herbs. Serve with flatbread.

Per serving: 148 kcalories, protein 9g, carbohydrate 17g, fat 5g, saturated fat 1g, fibre 6g, sugar none, salt 1.07g

Serves 4 ▪ prep 5 mins ▪ cook 20 mins

1 tbsp olive oil
1 medium onion, chopped
2 celery sticks, chopped
2 tsp ground cumin
600ml/1 pint vegetable stock
400g can chopped tomatoes
    with garlic
410g can chickpeas, rinsed and
    drained
100g/4oz frozen broad beans
zest and juice ½ lemon
large handful fresh coriander or
    parsley leaves, to serve

Lamb hotpot soup ❅

Pearl barley is a great filler for soups and stews. As it cooks it will help to thicken the soup.

Serves 4 ■ prep 10 mins ■ cook 25 mins

1 tsp olive oil
200g/8oz lamb neck fillet, trimmed of fat and cut into small pieces
½ large onion, finely chopped
50g/2oz pearl barley
600g/1lb 5oz root vegetables (we used potato, parsnip and swede), chopped into small cubes
2 tsp Worcestershire sauce
1 litre/1¾ pints lamb or beef stock
1 fresh thyme sprig
100g/4oz frozen green beans, finely chopped

1 Heat the oil in a large pan. Season the lamb and fry for a few mins until well browned. Add the onion and barley then fry gently for 1 min. Add the root veg and cook for 2 mins, then add the Worcestershire sauce, stock and thyme, and simmer, covered, for 20 mins.

2 With 5 mins to go, add the green beans. Once everything is cooked, put a quarter of the soup into a separate bowl and purée with a stick blender (or in a food processor), then stir back into the rest of the soup. Ladle into four bowls and serve with granary bread.

Per serving: 236 kcalories, protein 16g, carbohydrate 24.4g, fat 9g, saturated fat 3.7g, fibre 4.7g, sugar 11g, salt 1.48g

Rich tomato soup with pesto ❅

There's no reason not to enjoy homemade tomato soup in the depths of winter. Choose a fresh pesto to finish the dish off.

Serves 4 ■ prep 10 mins ■ cook 15 mins

1 tbsp butter or olive oil
2 garlic cloves, crushed
5 sundried or SunBlush tomatoes in oil, roughly chopped
3 × 400g cans plum tomatoes in tomato juice
500ml/18fl oz vegetable stock
1 tsp sugar
142ml pot soured cream
125g/4½oz fresh basil pesto
small handful fresh basil leaves, to serve

1 Heat the butter or oil in a large pan, then add the garlic and soften for a few mins over a low heat. Add all the tomatoes, the stock, sugar and seasoning, then bring to a simmer. Let the soup bubble for 10 mins until the tomatoes have broken down a little.

2 Blend with a stick blender, adding half the pot of soured cream as you go. Taste and adjust the seasoning – add more sugar if you need to. Serve in bowls with 1 tbsp of the pesto swirled on top, a little more soured cream and scattered with basil leaves.

Per serving: 213 kcalories, protein 8g, carbohydrate 14g, fat 14g, saturated fat 7g, fibre 4g, sugar 13g, salt 1.15g

Perfect pancakes ❄

Make a stack of these and freeze them — they are ideal for emergency puddings.

1 Put the flour and a pinch of salt into a mixing bowl and make a well in the centre. Crack the eggs into the middle, then pour in about 50ml of milk and 1 tbsp of oil. Start whisking from the centre, gradually drawing the flour into the eggs, milk and oil. Once all the flour is incorporated, beat until you have a smooth, thick paste. Add a little more milk if it is too stiff to beat.

2 While still whisking, pour in a steady stream of the remaining milk. Continue pouring and whisking until you have a batter that is the consistency of slightly thick single cream.

3 Heat a pan over a moderate heat, then wipe it with a sheet of oiled kitchen paper. Ladle some batter into the pan, tilting the pan to move the mixture around for a thin and even layer. Leave to cook, undisturbed, for about 30 secs. If the pan is the right temperature, the pancake should turn golden underneath after about 30 secs and will be ready to turn.

4 Holding the pan handle, ease a fish slice under the pancake, then quickly flip it over. Make sure the pancake is lying flat against the base of the pan with no folds, then cook for another 30 secs before turning out on to a warm plate. Continue with the rest of the batter, serving the pancakes as you cook them or stack them on to a plate. You can freeze the pancakes for 1 month wrapped in cling film.

Per pancake: 107 kcalories, protein 4g, carbohydrate 12g, fat 5g, saturated fat 1g, fibre none, sugar 2g, salt 0.10g

TIP Make pancake toppings from whatever you have to hand. Lemon and sugar, blueberries and maple syrup, grated chocolate, or fresh berries and sweetened cream.

Serves 8 ▪ prep 10–15 mins ▪ cook 8–10 mins

100g/4oz plain flour
2 eggs
300ml/½ pint milk
1 tbsp sunflower oil, plus extra for frying

Cookie-dough crumble

An easy-to-make treat that kids will love.

Heat oven to 220C/fan 200C/gas 7. Tip the still-frozen fruit into a shallow baking dish and scatter torn pieces of the dough all over the top. Bake for 20 mins until crisp and golden. Serve with cream, ice cream or custard.

Per serving: 457 kcalories, protein 8g, carbohydrate 57g, fat 24g, saturated fat 13g, fibre 6g, added sugar 9g, salt 1.2g

Serves 4 ▪ prep 5 mins ▪ cook 20 mins

500g bag mixed frozen fruit
350g fresh cookie dough

Easy rice pud

A low-fat rice pudding, but no skimping on creaminess.

1   Heat oven to 150C/fan 130C/gas 2. Wash the rice and drain well. Butter an 850ml ovenproof baking dish, then tip in the rice and sugar and stir through the milk.

2   Sprinkle over the nutmeg and top with the bay leaf or lemon zest. Cook for 2 hours or until the pudding wobbles ever so slightly when shaken.

Per serving: 214 kcalories, protein 8.1g, carbohydrate 40.2g, fat 3.5g, saturated fat 1.8g, fibre none, sugar 21.3g, salt 0.19g

Serves 4 ▪ prep 5 mins ▪ cook 2 hours

100g/4oz pudding rice
50g/2oz sugar
700ml/1¼ pints milk
pinch of grated nutmeg
1 bay leaf or a little lemon zest

Homemade custard

Good custard is simple to make from scratch.

1 Scrape the seeds from 1 vanilla pod. Put the milk in a pan and add the vanilla pod and seeds. Slowly bring to the boil then take off the heat and leave to stand.

2 Whisk the egg yolks and whole egg with the caster sugar until pale and thick. Whisk in the milk then strain into a clean pan and put back on a low heat, stirring continuously until the custard thickens. Stir in the double cream and serve.

Per serving: 369 kcalories, protein 6.3g, carbohydrate 20.2g, fat 29.8g, saturated fat 14.8g, fibre none, sugar 20.2g, salt 0.13g

Serves 6 ▪ prep 10 mins ▪ cook 10 mins

1 vanilla pod
250ml/9fl oz milk
5 egg yolks and 1 whole egg
100g/4oz caster sugar
250ml/9fl oz double cream

Quick chocolate sauce

An indulgent chocolate sauce that is perfect for pouring over vanilla ice cream.

1 In a pan, bring the cream, milk and cinnamon to the boil. Take the pan off the heat and add the chocolate. Stir until the chocolate has melted. Serve at once, or reheat gently when ready to use.

Per serving: 484 kcalories, protein 5.6g, carbohydrate 25.2g, fat 40.8g, saturated fat 21.9g, fibre 2.9g, sugar 16.3g, salt 0.06g

TIP For an even speedier chocolate sauce: mix 300g/10oz ready-made custard with 25g/1oz plain chocolate. Warm the custard in a pan, stir in the chocolate chunks until melted then pour over ice cream.

Serves 6 ▪ Prep 2 mins ▪ cook 5–10 mins

200g/8oz good-quality plain
  chocolate, chopped
142ml pot double cream
150ml/¼ pint full-fat milk
pinch of ground cinnamon

10 super-quick storecupboard ideas

Never throw away food again – you can always find a use for scraps and half-finished packs. Here are some quick ideas for some common leftover ingredients.

■ **Herb butter**

Chop leftover herbs and mix into softened butter. Dollop on to a piece of cling film, roll into a cylinder, twist the ends and freeze. Simply slice off rounds and use to top meat, fish or poultry.

■ **Banana smoothies**

Peel over-ripe bananas, then wrap tightly in cling film and freeze (you can freeze them for up to 1 month). Cut 1 frozen banana into chunks, then put in a blender with ½ glass orange juice, 150g pot natural yogurt and 1 tsp clear honey. Blend until smooth.

■ **Carrot muffins**

In a large bowl, stir together 200g/8oz self-raising flour and 200g/8oz caster sugar with 1 tsp baking powder and 1 tsp ground cinnamon. In a jug, beat 150ml/2½fl oz milk and 150ml/2½fl oz sunflower oil with 2 eggs. Mix with the dry ingredients along with 2 grated carrots and 50g/1oz sultanas, stirring briefly. Divide among 12 muffin cases and bake for 15–20 mins at 180C/ fan 160C/gas 4 until risen and golden.

■ **Meaty pizza**

Put 50g/1oz sliced chorizo or spicy salami, ½ thinly sliced red pepper and a liberal sprinkling of dried chilli flakes on top of one medium Margherita pizza before baking. Scatter with a handful of olives, if you have them, to serve.

■ **Quick raita dip**

Stir together 150g pot natural yogurt and 85g/3oz mayonnaise along with a large pinch of salt and black pepper. Coarsely grate a large chunk of cucumber then squeeze out the excess liquid and add to the yogurt mix with a generous amount of finely shredded basil.

■ **Quick quesadilla**

Sandwich shredded turkey, thinly sliced red onion and grated cheddar between two tortillas. Pan-fry, turning halfway, until the tortillas are crisp and cheese melted. Cut into wedges and serve with tomato salsa.

■ **Cheat's French onion soup**

Cook 4 chopped onions in 25g/1oz butter and 1 tbsp olive oil until soft and well browned, about 20 mins. Add 1 tsp Dijon mustard and 2 x 400g cans beef consommé, and simmer for 5 mins. Pour into bowls and top with slices of melted cheese on toast.

■ **Perk up houmous**

Cook 200g/8oz frozen peas in boiling water for 2 mins then blend together with 200g/8oz houmous. Add a little fresh lemon juice and a pinch of ground cumin to taste, season then serve with warm pitta bread or toast.

■ **Tomato and mustard dressing**

Whisk together 2 tsp tomato purée, 1 tsp Dijon mustard, 6 tbsp olive oil and 2 tbsp balsamic vinegar. Add a little salt and pepper to taste and use to dress green leaves.

■ **Quick icing**

In a food processor, blitz 8 large strawberries, then sieve. Mix with 300g/10oz icing sugar and use to top cakes and buns.

chapter 5

Weekend feasts

At the weekend, you will hopefully have a little more time to spend in the kitchen. In this chapter we have collected some delicious recipes for starters, mains, sides and desserts that are perfect for family and friends or for a leisurely weekend lunch or supper.

The recipes in this chapter are for you to mix and match to suit your mood or the occasion. Some of the ingredients are a little more expensive than those used elsewhere in the book, but if you buy the ingredients in season, when they are at their most abundant, they will be cheaper. You can of course make any of the recipes here all year round, but whenever possible, try to buy locally to reduce your carbon footprint.

We've also included some simple baking recipes and stocks. Once you are practised in the art of bread making you can bake these recipes quickly during the week; if you're not an experienced baker, save these recipes, along with the homemade stocks, for when you are not so rushed. Homemade bread is not only delicious eaten fresh and still warm from the oven, but also freezes well, so you can make a batch of loaves at the weekend and freeze them for later in the month. Stocks also freeze well, provided the meat or fish ingredients have not been frozen before so, again, make these at the weekend and freeze to use at a later date instead of a stock cube.

■ If you want to keep it simple (and cheap) serve a few nibbles, like olives or crudités, with a bought or homemade dip. But if you've got time and want to impress, here's a selection of smart but easy starters to serve instead.

Tomato and basil granita ❄

An iced starter may seem strange, but try it and you'll see how delicious it is.

Serves 8 ■ prep 25 mins, plus macerating

900g/2lb very ripe tomatoes
1 tsp salt
1 garlic clove, finely chopped
1 tsp ground black pepper
1 tbsp red wine vinegar
bunch fresh basil leaves

TIP A granita makes a fantastic, low-fat and refreshing end to a meal too. Make it with berries, watermelon or citrus fruits.

1 Chop the tomatoes and put in a bowl with all the other ingredients except the basil leaves. If you have time, leave them to macerate at room temperature overnight. Put a high-sided metal tray in the freezer to chill.

2 Blitz the tomatoes in a blender (you will need to do this in batches) then strain through a fine sieve. Shred the basil leaves and stir through. Pour the liquid into the chilled tray, cover with cling film and freeze. Once frozen around the edges and slushy in the middle, use a fork to break up the ice into smaller crystals. Repeat the breaking-up process every half hour (at least three times) until it's completely frozen and the texture of snow. Return the tray to the freezer until ready to serve.

Per serving: 30 kcalories, protein 1g, carbohydrate 6g, fat none, saturated fat none, fibre 1g, sugar 6g, salt 0.65g

Goat's cheese, spring onion and parsley soufflés

These soufflés are a useful recipe to have to hand. Ever popular, they can be enjoyed time and again.

1   Heat oven to 190C/fan 170C/gas 5. Butter six 150ml ramekins or ovenproof dishes. Set the dishes on a baking sheet to make them easier to remove from the oven. Melt the butter in a heavy-based pan, stir in the flour and cook, stirring, for 1 min. Slowly mix in the milk to make a thick sauce. Simmer for 2 mins to cook the flour. Remove from the heat and stir in the parsley, spring onions, goat's cheese, egg yolks, 3 tbsp of the parmesan and seasoning.

2   Whisk the egg whites until they are stiff, then fold into the sauce in three batches, cutting through the mixture with a metal spoon each time to incorporate the egg white without losing too much air from the mix. Divide among the prepared dishes and sprinkle with the remaining parmesan. Bake for 20 mins until risen and golden. Serve immediately.

Per serving 218 kcalories, protein 12.9g, carbohydrate 5.5g, fat 16.2g, saturated fat 9.2g, fibre 0.5g, sugar 2.3g, salt 0.77g

Serves 6 ▪ prep 20 mins ▪ cook 25 mins

25g/1oz butter, plus extra for greasing
25g/1oz plain flour
200ml/7fl oz milk
generous bunch fresh parsley, finely chopped
bunch spring onions, finely chopped
150g pack goat's cheese, chopped into small chunks
3 eggs, separated
4 tbsp grated parmesan

Steamed mussels with leeks, thyme and bacon

Bring bistro-style to your dinner party with this cheap but impressive first course.

Serves 2 ▪ prep 20 mins ▪ cook 15 mins

750g/1lb 10oz mussels
25g/1oz butter
6 rashers smoked streaky bacon, chopped into small pieces
2 small leeks, sliced on the diagonal
handful fresh thyme sprigs
small glass cider or white wine

1 Scrub and de-beard the mussels. Discard any that don't close when tapped on the edge of the sink. Heat half the butter in a pan, then sizzle the bacon for 3–4 mins until starting to brown. Add the leeks and thyme, then sweat everything together for 4–5 mins until soft. Turn the heat up high, add the mussels and cider or wine, then cover and cook for 4–5 mins, shaking the pan occasionally, until the mussels have opened. Discard any that don't open.

2 Scoop the mussels and other bits into a dish using a slotted spoon, then place the pan back on the heat. Boil the juices for 1 min with the rest of the butter, then pour over the mussels and serve with crusty bread.

Per serving: 377 kcalories, protein 24g, carbohydrate 9g, fat 26g, saturated fat 12g, fibre 2g, sugar 5g, salt 2.76g

Cheesy autumn mushrooms

A light seasonal start to lunch or supper that can be made ahead, then popped in the oven when ready to serve.

Serves 4 ▪ prep 5 mins ▪ cook 10 mins

4 large field mushrooms
100g/4oz gorgonzola or other blue cheese, crumbled
25g/1oz walnuts, toasted and roughly chopped
4 fresh thyme sprigs
knob of butter, cut into small pieces
rocket leaves, to serve

1 Heat oven to 200C/fan 180C/gas 6. Arrange the mushrooms on a baking sheet. Scatter over the cheese, walnuts, thyme sprigs and butter. You can prepare up to this step a day in advance.

2 Pop in the oven and cook for 10 mins until the cheese is melted and the mushrooms are softened. Arrange some rocket leaves on plates and put the mushrooms on top.

Per serving: 165 kcalories, protein 8.3g, carbohydrate 0.7g, fat 14.4g, saturated fat 6.6g, fibre 1.3g, sugar 0.4g, salt 0.96g.

Chicken liver and sherry pâté

Make the most of reasonably priced meat with this luxurious starter.

Serves 6–8 ■ prep 10 mins
■ cook 10 mins, plus chilling

500g/1lb 2oz chicken livers
100g/4oz butter
100g/4oz unsmoked lardons or
    chopped streaky bacon
1 garlic clove, crushed or finely
    chopped
1 tbsp fresh thyme leaves or
    1 tsp dried
5 tbsp dry sherry (but whatever
    you have is fine)
fresh herb such as rosemary,
    thyme or bay leaves, to garnish
toasted brioche or raisin bread,
    cornichons and sea salt, to serve

1 Rinse the chicken livers and cut away any dark patches and small stringy threads. Pat dry with kitchen paper. Heat 25g/1oz of the butter in a frying pan until foaming, then add the lardons or bacon and fry until crisp. Add the chicken livers, garlic and thyme and fry briskly for about 5 mins, until everything is evenly browned. The chicken livers should be nicely browned on the outside, but pink inside and should feel squashy when pressed.

2 Add the sherry, salt and pepper, then bubble for a few mins. Remove from the heat. Blitz the mixture in a food processor until smooth, then spoon into a jar or dish. Smooth the top.

3 Melt the remaining butter. Put a herb sprig or bay leaf on top of the pâté and pour over the butter, leaving the sediment behind. Leave to cool, then chill until set.

4 Serve spooned from the dish with toasted brioche or raisin bread, a bowl of cornichons and a little sea salt.

Per serving: 258 kcalories, protein 17.3g, carbohydrate 1.2g, fat 19.2g, saturated fat 10.7g, fibre none, sugar 0.9g, salt 0.93g

Tomato and caramelized onion tarte Tatin

The principle for making this savoury version of a tarte Tatin is the same as the classic dessert. It's also perfect for a light supper or starter.

1 For the caramelized onion, heat the butter and oil in a frying pan until the butter has melted. Tip in the onion and cook over a medium heat for about 10 mins until beautifully golden, stirring often. Stir in the sugar and cook for 2 mins. Tip the onion and juices into a bowl and set aside. Heat oven to 200C/fan 180C/gas 6.

2 For the pastry, rub the butter into the flour to make fine crumbs. Stir in the parmesan, thyme and a pinch of salt. Add the egg yolk and 2 tbsp cold water, then mix to make a dough. Wrap in cling film.

3 For the tomatoes, heat the butter and oil in a 20cm tarte Tatin tin on the hob until quite hot. Stir in the sugar and garlic, then put in the plum tomatoes cut-side down with a few thyme sprigs, and fry for no more than 1 min. Scatter in the whole cherry tomatoes and tuck in a bit more thyme. Take off the heat and spread the onions on top. Season with salt and pepper.

4 Roll out the pastry slightly bigger than the top of the tin. Lay it over the onions and tuck any excess down the sides.

5 Bake on a baking sheet for 25 mins until golden. Cool for 5 mins, invert a plate over the top and upturn the tart on to it. Scatter with extra thyme and freshly ground black pepper.

Per serving: 625 kcalories, protein 12g, carbohydrate 46g, fat 45g, saturated fat 29g, fibre 4g, added sugar 3g, salt 1.57g

Serves 4 ▪ prep 1–1¼ hours ▪ cook 25 mins

for the caramelized onion
50g/2oz butter
1 tbsp olive oil
1 large onion, cut into thin wedges
1 tsp sugar

for the pastry
85g/3oz butter
175g/6oz self-raising flour
50g/2oz parmesan, finely grated
small handful fresh thyme leaves
1 large egg yolk

for the tomatoes
25g/1oz butter
1 tbsp olive oil
1 tsp sugar
1 fat garlic clove, finely chopped
5 plum tomatoes, halved
    lengthways
several fresh thyme sprigs, plus
    extra for scattering
300g pack cherry tomatoes

■ There are recipes here for any time of the year; smart enough for a dinner and leisurely enough for a casual lunch.

Hot-smoked salmon salad with chilli lemon dressing

This delicious salad is thrown together in minutes to make a fresh, seasonal dish that's stylish enough for entertaining.

Serves 8 ■ prep 20 mins ■ cook 10 mins

for the salad
500g/1lb 2oz new potatoes, halved
200g pack asparagus tips
250g bag mixed salad leaves
bunches fresh parsley and mint leaves, roughly chopped
140g/5oz radishes, finely chopped
8 hot-smoked salmon steaks, skin removed
4 spring onions, chopped
for the dressing
3 tbsp lemon juice
125ml/4fl oz olive oil
1 tsp wholegrain mustard
2 red chillies, deseeded and finely chopped

1 Boil the potatoes in salted water for 10 mins until tender, adding the asparagus tips for the final 2 mins of cooking. Drain and allow to cool. Whisk together the dressing ingredients. Season to taste.

2 In a large bowl, toss together the potatoes, asparagus, salad leaves, herbs and radishes. Add two thirds of the dressing, thoroughly mix through the salad, then arrange on a large platter. Break the hot-smoked salmon into big chunks, then scatter over the top of the salad along with the spring onions. Pour the remaining dressing over the top, to serve.

Per serving: 299 kcalories, protein 21g, carbohydrate 13g, fat 19g, saturated fat 3g, fibre 2g, sugar 3g, salt 2.09g

Buttery trout with capers

Trout is a classic fish that goes wonderfully well with the salty sourness of the capers.

**Serves 4 ▪ prep 5 mins
▪ cook 10 mins**

4 thick trout fillets
100g/4oz butter
squeeze lemon juice
handful fresh parsley leaves,
   chopped
2 tbsp capers, rinsed
green beans, to serve

TIP You can turn this into a
veggie dish using halloumi
cheese instead of trout, if you
are entertaining vegetarians.
Heat a griddle pan until really
hot. Cut a 240g pack halloumi
cheese into 8 slices, then cook
for 2–3 mins on each side.
Remove from the pan and
keep warm. Pour in 4 tbsp
olive oil, the juice of ½ a lemon
and 2 tbsp of capers, then
warm through. Add 2 handfuls
of chopped mixed fresh herbs,
such as parsley and oregano,
to the pan just before serving.
Check the seasoning, then
drizzle the dressing over the
halloumi to serve.

1   Heat oven to 200C/fan 180C/gas 6. Rinse the fish, then pat dry
with kitchen paper. Put in a roasting tin, season with salt and pepper,
then dot with a third of the butter. Roast for 10–12 mins.

2   When the fish is almost ready, melt the remaining butter in a
frying pan. Turn up the heat until it turns brown then take off the
heat and add the lemon juice, parsley and capers. Pour over the fish,
and serve with green beans.

Per serving: 345 kcalories, protein 28g, carbohydrate 1g, fat 26g,
saturated fat 14g, fibre none, sugar none, salt 1.04g

Chilli prawn linguine

Teaming expensive ingredients like prawns with cheaper ones like pasta and tomatoes is a great way to keep costs down.

1 Mix the dressing ingredients in a small bowl, season with salt and pepper and set aside.

2 Cook the pasta according to the pack instructions. Add the sugar snap peas for the last min or so of cooking time.

3 Meanwhile, heat the oil in a wok or large frying pan, toss in the garlic and chilli, and cook over a fairly gentle heat for about 30 secs without letting the garlic brown. Tip in the prawns and cook over a high heat, stirring frequently, for about 3 mins until they turn pink.

4 Add the tomatoes and cook, stirring occasionally, for 3 mins until they just start to soften. Drain the pasta and sugar snaps well, then toss into the prawn mixture. Tear in the basil leaves, stir, and season with salt and pepper. Serve with the salad leaves, drizzled with the lime dressing and warm crusty bread.

Per serving: 333 kcalories, protein 32g, carbohydrate 42g, fat 5g, saturated fat 1g, fibre 3g, added sugar 2g, salt 0.9g

**Serves 6 ▪ prep 10 mins
▪ cook 10–15 mins**

300g/10oz linguine pasta
200g/8oz sugar snap peas, trimmed
2 tbsp olive oil
2 large garlic cloves, finely chopped
1 large red chilli, deseeded and finely chopped
24 raw king prawns, peeled
12 cherry tomatoes, halved
handful fresh basil leaves
mixed salad leaves and crusty white bread, to serve
for the lime dressing
2 tbsp fat-free fromage frais
zest and juice 2 limes
2 tsp golden caster sugar

Lincolnshire sausage and lentil simmer ❄

Sausages are great for the weekend and this dish is perfect for a casual lunch with friends.

Serves 6 ▪ prep 30–40 mins ▪ cook 45 mins

1 tbsp vegetable oil
130g pack cubed pancetta or bacon rashers (chopped if using bacon)
2 × 400g packs Lincolnshire pork sausages
2 onions, roughly chopped
1 large carrot, chopped into small pieces
4 garlic cloves, roughly chopped
3 fresh rosemary sprigs
300g/10oz Puy lentils
850ml/1½ pints chicken stock
1 tbsp white wine vinegar
400g can chopped tomatoes
2 tbsp fresh parsley, chopped

1   Heat the oil in a large flameproof casserole dish or very large pan with a lid. Add the pancetta and sausages, and sizzle for 10 mins, turning the sausages occasionally until browned and sticky. Scoop the sausages out on to a plate.

2   Add the onions, carrot and garlic to the pancetta, and continue to cook for 3–4 mins until the onions soften. Return the sausages to the pan and add the rosemary, lentils, stock, vinegar and tomatoes, then season with salt and pepper. Bring to the boil and simmer rapidly without the lid for 5 mins, then lower the heat, cover and simmer for 45 mins, stirring occasionally until the lentils are tender. Check the seasoning, scatter over the parsley and serve from the pan with seasonal green veg.

Per serving: 640 kcalories, protein 39g, carbohydrate 37g, fat 37g, saturated fat 13g, fibre 6g, added sugar none, salt 4.24g

Fresh lasagne with pesto

A easy-to-prepare, meat-free recipe with authentic Italian flavours.

1   Preheat oven to 200C/gas 6/fan 180C. Put the milk, butter and flour in a pan and cook over a medium heat, whisking until thickened and smooth. Simmer for 1 minute. Take off the heat, season and add the nutmeg. Cool, stirring occasionally to stop a skin forming.

2   Put the spinach in a large heatproof bowl, pour over a kettle full of boiling water and leave for 30 seconds. Drain into a colander, cool under the cold tap then squeeze it well to remove the excess liquid.

3   Spread a spoonful or two of the sauce on the bottom of a large ovenproof dish (about 30x20cm) and lay a third of the lasagne on top. Spoon over a third of the sauce and spread it out. Swirl a spoonful of pesto through the sauce with a knife and scatter over half the spinach with a third of the tomatoes, a few basil leaves and a third of the cheeses. Season with salt and pepper. Layer another third of the lasagne with a third of the sauce, a spoonful of pesto, the rest of the spinach, a third of the tomatoes and cheeses and some basil. Season.

4   Finish with a layer of lasagne, the last of the sauce, pesto, cheeses and the tomatoes, including those on the vine. Bake for 35–40 minutes until golden. Scatter with the last of the basil leaves and serve.

Per serving: 711 kcalories, protein 38g, carbohydrate 46g, fat 43g, saturated fat 25g, fibre 4g, added sugar none, salt 2.5g

Serves 6 ▪ prep 30 mins ▪ cook 35–40 mins

1.2 litres/2 pints milk
100g/4oz butter, cut into pieces
100g/4oz plain flour
pinch of freshly grated nutmeg
500g/1lb 2oz baby spinach leaves
250g/9oz fresh lasagne sheets
3 rounded tbsp pesto
500g/1lb 2oz cherry tomatoes on the vine, two vines left whole
good handful fresh basil leaves
175g/6oz parmesan, coarsely grated
2 x 150g balls mozzarella, preferably buffalo, torn into bite-sized pieces

Spinach roulade with Boursin and sundried tomatoes

Although this is simple to make, you need to work quickly at the end to make sure that it is still warm when you serve it.

1 Heat oven to 190C/fan 170C/gas 5 and line a Swiss roll tin (23x32cm) with non-stick baking parchment. Cook the spinach in the microwave according to pack instructions (about 2 mins for each bag), then, when cool enough to handle, squeeze out as much juice as you can. Tip the spinach into a food processor or blender and add the egg yolks, 1 tbsp of fromage frais, plenty of seasoning and the flour. Blend until it is really finely chopped and well mixed.

2 Whisk the egg whites until stiff, then fold into the spinach mixture. Spread in the tin and bake for 12–15 mins until firm to the touch.

3 Meanwhile, beat the rest of the fromage frais into the Boursin or roulé until creamy. Put a sheet of baking parchment on the work surface and dust with a little of the parmesan.

4 Turn the spinach mixture on to the sheet of parmesan-dusted baking parchment and carefully peel off the parchment stuck to the cooked spinach mixture. Spread with the cheese mix and scatter over the tomatoes. Roll up from the shortest end using the paper to guide you. Serve straight away.

Per serving: 441 kcalories, protein 21g, carbohydrate 16g, fat 33g, saturated fat 15g, fibre 4g, sugar 6g, salt 2.08g

Serves 4 ▪ prep 20 mins ▪ cook 15 mins

2 x 200g bags ready-washed spinach
5 large eggs, separated
200g pot fromage frais (not the virtually fat-free one)
3 tbsp self-raising flour
150g pack garlic and herb Boursin or roulé
finely grated parmesan, for dusting
10–12 sundried tomatoes, shredded

Leek and sage risotto with crisp bacon

Meat is expensive these days, this is a great entertaining dish that doesn't rely on it – the bacon is all you need.

Serves 4 ▪ prep 10 mins
▪ cook 20 mins

1 tbsp olive oil
2 leeks, sliced
4 fresh sage leaves, shredded, or pinch dried
350g/12 oz arborio risotto rice
small glass white wine
1.5 litres/3½ pints vegetable stock
2–3 rashers streaky bacon
3 tbsp grated parmesan

1　Heat the oil in a pan, add the leeks and sage, and fry for 2 mins until the leeks are softened. Stir in the rice and cook for 1 min. Add the wine and one third of the stock. Bring to the boil and set the timer for 20 mins. Simmer, stirring occasionally, until the stock has been absorbed, then add half the remaining stock and carry on cooking, stirring a bit more frequently, until it has been absorbed. Pour in the last of the stock, stir, then simmer until cooked and creamy.

2　Meanwhile, grill the bacon until golden and crisp. Remove the rice from the heat, then stir in 2 tbsp of the parmesan and some freshly ground pepper. Spoon on to a plate, sprinkle with the remaining parmesan and top with the bacon.

Per serving: 685 kcalories, protein 27g, carbohydrate 81g, fat 27g, saturated fat 9g, fibre 8g, sugar 13g, salt 1.65g

Slow-cooked lamb with onions and thyme

Beloved of gastro-pubs, this gutsy recipe makes meltingly tender meat and is satisfyingly rich.

Serves 4 ▪ prep 15 mins
▪ cook 3 hours 10 mins

½ leg of lamb (about 1.25kg/2lb 12oz)
3 tbsp olive oil
1kg/2lb 4oz onions (about 4 large ones)
handful fresh thyme sprigs
300ml/½ pint red wine
large handful fresh parsley leaves, chopped

1　Heat oven to 160C/fan 140C/gas 3. Wipe the meat all over and season well. Heat the olive oil in a large, heavy flameproof casserole dish, add the meat and fry over a high heat for about 8 mins, turning until it is evenly browned. Remove to a plate.

2　Thinly slice the onions. Add to the pan and fry for about 10 mins, until softened and tinged brown. Add a few of the thyme sprigs and cook for 1–2 mins. Season with salt and pepper.

3　Sit the lamb on top of the onions, then add the wine. Cover and bake for 3 hours. You can make the casserole up to this step two days in advance, and reheat for 45 mins when required. To finish off, strip the leaves from two of the thyme sprigs, chop and mix with the parsley leaves. Scatter over before serving.

Per serving: 731 kcalories, protein 63g, carbohydrate 21g, fat 39g, saturated fat 19g, fibre 4g, added sugar none, salt 0.87g

Pumpkin curry with chickpeas and spinach ❄

This stands alone as a vegan main course but also makes a complex side dish to serve with spiced roast meat or fish.

Serves 4 as a main course
■ **prep 20 mins** ■ **cook 20 mins**

1 tbsp sunflower oil
2–3 tbsp Thai yellow curry paste
2 onions, finely chopped
3 large fresh lemongrass stalks, bashed with the back of a knife
6 cardamom pods
1 tbsp mustard seeds
1 piece pumpkin or 1 small squash (about 1kg/2lb 4oz)
250ml/9fl oz vegetable stock
400ml can reduced-fat coconut milk
410g can chickpeas, drained and rinsed
2 limes
large handful fresh mint leaves, chopped, and naan bread, to serve

1   Heat the oil in a pan, then gently fry the curry paste with the onions, lemongrass, cardamom and mustard seeds for 2–3 mins until aromatic. Stir the pumpkin or squash into the pan and coat in the paste, and pour in the stock and coconut milk. Bring to a simmer, add the chickpeas, then cook for about 10 mins until the pumpkin is tender. The curry can now be cooled and frozen for up to 1 month.

2   Squeeze the juice of 1 lime into the curry, then cut the other lime into wedges to serve alongside. Just before serving, tear over mint leaves, then bring to the table with the lime wedges and warm naan breads.

Per serving: 293 kcalories, protein 9g, carbohydrate 26g, fat 18g, saturated fat 10g, fibre 7g, sugar 10g, salt 1.32g

Braised pork with prunes

A delicious and comforting pork lunch or supper that takes minutes to prepare.

1   Heat the olive oil in a flameproof casserole dish and cook the pork, turning occasionally, until it is golden brown all over, about 10 mins (you need plenty of space in the pan, so cook in two batches if the meat starts to steam). Remove from the pan to a plate. Tip out any burnt bits, then add the butter and cook the onion for 3–5 mins until softened.

2   Stir in the flour, then return the pork and any juices to the pan. Pour over the wine and enough stock to cover the meat. Bring to the boil, reduce to a simmer, put the lid on and cook for 45 mins, stirring occasionally. Tip in the prunes, top up with stock or water to cover the meat, and cook for 45 mins more, uncovered, until really tender. Serve sprinkled with parsley and serve with cooked pasta.

Per serving: 497 kcalories, protein 29g, carbohydrate 22g, fat 28g, saturated fat 10g, fibre 1g, added sugar none, salt 0.54g

Serves 4 ▪ prep 10 mins
▪ cook 1 hour 50 mins

1 tbsp olive oil
600g/1lb 5oz pork shoulder,
    roughly cut into 5cm/2in chunks
small knob of butter
1 onion, sliced
1 tbsp plain flour
2 large glasses white wine
300ml/½ pint chicken stock
140g/5oz dried prunes (about 12)
handful fresh parsley, chopped,
    to sprinkle

Braised oxtail with basil dumplings

You need to braise oxtail for a good few hours. What you are then left with is the magic of cooking – soft, melting meat with a thick, glistening sauce.

**Serves 6 ■ prep 20 mins
■ cook 4½–5 hours**

2 tbsp plain flour
2 oxtails, jointed and cut into
   pieces
4 tbsp sunflower oil
2 onions, chopped
3 carrots, chopped into chunks
2 celery sticks, cut into small
   chunks
2 garlic cloves, chopped
2 tbsp tomato purée
a few bay leaves and fresh
   thyme sprigs, tied together
   with fine string
75cl bottle full-bodied red wine
1 beef stock cube
for the dumplings
300g/10oz self-raising flour
bunch fresh basil, leaves removed,
   (reserve a few, to garnish)
85g/3oz butter
3 egg whites
olive oil, for drizzling

1 Heat oven to 180C/fan 160C/gas 4. Season the flour with salt and pepper, then toss the oxtail in it until evenly coated. Heat the oil in a large flameproof casserole dish. Working in batches, brown the meat really well on all sides. Remove from the pan, then add the veg and garlic, and fry for 3–4 mins until starting to colour. Stir in the tomato purée and herbs. Tip the meat back into the pan, pour over the wine, then crumble in the stock cube. Season, cover the pan and braise in the oven for 4–5 hours until the meat is meltingly tender. You can make this up to 2 days ahead and keep chilled in the fridge. Scoop any fat off the top with a spoon before reheating.

2 To make the dumplings, tip the flour and basil into a food processor with a generous pinch of salt, then blitz until the basil is finely chopped. Add the butter and blitz until it's the texture of breadcrumbs, then gradually add the egg whites until everything comes together. On a floured surface, roll the dumplings into small, walnut-size balls, then cover with a tea towel until ready to cook.

3 To serve, bring a large pan of salted water to the boil. Simmer the dumplings for 15 mins, then remove with a slotted spoon. While the dumplings are cooking, gently reheat the meat in the sauce. Serve a few chunks of meat in a soup bowl with a few dumplings, drizzled with olive oil and scattered with basil leaves.

Per serving: 812 kcalories, protein 53g, carbohydrate 50g, fat 41g, saturated fat 17g, fibre 4g, sugar 8g, salt 2.08g

TIP If you are cooking with wine, use a fairly good one to give your dish the best flavour. Serve a similar-style wine with the meal to give a well-rounded flavour.

Lamb shanks with chickpeas and Moroccan spices

The subtle flavour of couscous goes well with North African flavours.

Serves 4 ▪ prep 1¼–1½ hours, plus soaking for chickpeas ▪ cook 2½–3 hours

175g/6oz dried chickpeas
2 tbsp olive oil
4 medium lamb shanks
2 medium onions, chopped
small knob root ginger, finely grated
3 garlic cloves, finely chopped
2 fresh green chillies, deseeded and finely chopped
2 tsp ground cumin
2 tsp dried coriander
1 tsp freshly ground black pepper
1 tsp paprika
2 large tomatoes, peeled, deseeded and chopped
850ml boiling water
pinch of saffron strands
2cm/¾in piece cinnamon stick
450g/1lb carrots, chopped into thick slices
140g/5oz ready-to-eat dried apricots
1 tsp clear honey
50g/2oz blanched almonds, fried in butter until browned and fresh coriander, chopped, to garnish

1 Soak the chickpeas overnight. Drain, tip into a pan and cover generously with cold water. Bring to the boil, simmer for 45 mins and drain.

2 Heat the oil in a large casserole dish and brown the lamb all over. Remove and set aside. Pour off most of the fat, leaving 1 tbsp in the dish, add the onions and fry for 8–10 mins until soft.

3 Heat oven to 160C/fan 140C/gas 3. Mix together the ginger, garlic, chillies, cumin, coriander, pepper and paprika. Add half of this to the onions, tip in the tomatoes and cook for 2–3 mins. Add the lamb and chickpeas, cover generously with the boiling water, bring to the boil and simmer for 5 mins. Cover and cook in the oven for 1½–2 hours until the chickpeas are really tender. You can prepare the dish up to this stage the day before. If you do, cool, cover and chill then bring back to simmering point before starting step 4.

4 Remove from the oven and stir in the remaining spice mixture, the saffron and cinnamon, carrots, apricots, honey and season with salt. Cover and return to the oven for 45 mins–1 hour until the lamb is tender and the vegetables cooked. Scatter the almonds and coriander on top and serve.

Per serving 653 kcalories, protein 50g, carbohydrate 55g, fat 27g, saturated fat 10g, fibre 11g, added sugar 1g, salt 0.47g

TIP: You can use canned chickpeas but as they are already cooked, start at step 2 and omit the chickpeas in step 3, adding just 425ml water. Drain and rinse 410g of canned chickpeas and add at the beginning of step 4.

■   The weekend is the perfect time to cook a big roast for everyone to sit down together and enjoy as part of a long, lazy lunch.

Foolproof slow-roast chicken

Slow roasting is a great way to keep the chicken moist. Adding the potatoes to the roasting tin infuses them with plenty of flavour, too.

**Serves 4 ■ prep 15 mins
■ cook 2 hours 20 mins**

butter, for greasing
1.6kg/3lb 8oz chicken
1kg/2lb 4oz roasting potatoes,
   halved or quartered if large
2 whole garlic bulbs, halved
   through the middle
100ml/3½fl oz white wine
100ml/3½fl oz chicken stock
2 fresh rosemary stems, broken
   into sprigs
6 bay leaves
1 lemon, cut into wedges

1   Heat oven to 160C/fan 140C/gas 3. Brush a large roasting tin all over with butter and smear some over the skin of the chicken.

2   Put the chicken in the tin and arrange the potatoes around it. Put the halved garlic bulbs in the tin, pour over the white wine and stock, then cover with foil and put in the oven. Cook for 1 hour then remove the foil and give the potatoes a shake. Add the herbs and lemon wedges, then cook uncovered for 50 mins.

3   Turn up the heat to 220C/fan 200C/gas 7. Cook for 30 mins more, then remove the chicken and potatoes from the pan. Cover the chicken loosely with foil and leave to rest on a plate for at least 10 mins before carving. Keep the potatoes warm. Serve with any pan juices.

Per serving: 634 kcalories, protein 44g, carbohydrate 56g, fat 27g, saturated fat 9g, fibre 5g, sugar 4g, salt 1.76g

Pot-roasted brisket in beer with parsnips and mushrooms

A great winter warmer, using an old-fashioned cut of beef.

Serves 6–8 ■ prep 25–35 mins ■ cook 2½–3 hours

about 1.25kg/2lb 12oz boned and rolled brisket
5 tbsp vegetable oil
large knob of butter
2 large onions, halved and chopped
2–3 celery sticks, finely chopped
2 carrots, chopped
250g/9oz large flat mushrooms, stalks chopped and heads thickly sliced
550ml bottle brown ale or stout
few fresh thyme sprigs
2 bay leaves
1–2 tsp light muscovado sugar
500g/1lb 2oz parsnips, cut into wedges
1 tbsp Dijon mustard
small handful fresh parsley or thyme leaves, chopped, to garnish

1   Heat oven to 190C/fan 170C/gas 5. Wash and dry the brisket and season. Heat 2 tbsp of the oil in a deep flameproof casserole dish and brown beef all over. Remove from the dish. Lower the heat, add the butter and fry the onions, celery, carrots and mushroom stalks for 6–8 mins.

2   Return the beef to the dish and add the beer, thyme, bay leaves and sugar. Add water if necessary so the liquid comes about two-thirds up the beef. Season, bring to a simmer, cover, and cook in the oven for 20 mins. Reduce the heat to 160C/fan 140C/gas 3 and cook for 2 hours, turning twice, until tender.

3   An hour before the beef is done, toss the parsnips in the remaining oil, season and roast on a baking sheet above the beef for 50 mins–1 hour until tender, turning once.

4   Turn up the oven to 190C/fan 170C/gas 5. Lift out the beef, cover with foil and keep warm. Stir the parsnips and mushroom caps into the beef juices in the casserole dish. Check the seasoning and add water if needed. Cover and return the dish to the oven for 20–25 mins until the mushrooms are tender.

5   To serve, use a slotted spoon to remove the vegetables and arrange them round the beef. Spoon off the excess fat from the juices, and whisk in the mustard then pour into a jug. Moisten the beef with a little juice and scatter with parsley or thyme to serve.

Per serving (6): 575 kcalories protein 34g, carbohydrate 20g, fat 39g, saturated fat 14g, fibre 5g, added sugar 1g, salt 0.53g

Greek roast lamb

Lamb is often at its best a bit later in the year.

**Serves 8 ▪ prep 15 mins
▪ cook about 1¾ hours**

1 large leg of lamb (about
   3kg/6lb 8oz)
6 garlic cloves
bunch fresh oregano leaves
zest and juice 1 lemon
6 tbsp olive oil
1.5kg/3lb 5oz new potatoes
400g can chopped tomatoes
large handful pitted baby
   Kalamata olives
green salad, to serve

1 Heat oven to 240C/fan 220C/gas 9. Pound the garlic, half the oregano, lemon zest and a pinch of salt in a pestle and mortar, then add the lemon juice and a drizzle of olive oil. Stab the lamb all over with a sharp knife then push the herb paste into the holes.

2 Tip the potatoes into a roasting tin, then toss in the remaining olive oil and any remaining herb paste. Nestle the lamb among the potatoes, roast for 20 mins, then reduce the temperature to 180C/fan 160C/gas 4. Roast for 1¼ hours for medium-rare, adding another 15 mins if you prefer your lamb medium. Baste the lamb once or twice with the juices and toss the potatoes. When the lamb is done to your liking, remove from the tin to rest. Add the remaining oregano to the potatoes, scoop from the tin and keep warm.

3 Put the roasting tin over a medium heat, add the tomatoes and olives to the pan juices. Simmer for a few mins. Serve the lamb, potatoes and sauce with a simple salad.

Per serving: 685 kcalories, protein 59g, carbohydrate 32g, fat 36g, saturated fat 14g, fibre 3g, sugar 4g, salt 0.54g

Roast pork with pear sauce

Pork works really well with pears. Try the sauce with game or duck.

**Serves 6 ▪ prep 20 mins
▪ cook 1 hour 50 mins**

2kg/4lb 8oz loin of pork, on the
   bone
2 tbsp sunflower oil
for the sauce
25g/1oz butter
4 ripe pears, peeled, cored and
   chopped into chunks
1 tbsp fennel seeds
150ml/¼ pint perry or dry cider
2 tbsp golden caster sugar

1 Heat oven to 240C/fan 220C/gas 9. Dry the skin of the pork with kitchen paper, then rub with the oil and season generously with sea salt. Sit in a roasting tin, then roast for 20 mins. Reduce the heat to 190C/fan 170C/gas 5 and continue to roast the pork for 1 hour 20 mins until cooked and the skin has turned to crisp crackling. If the skin isn't crisp enough, turn the oven back up to 240C/fan 220C/gas 9 for a further 10 mins.

2 While the pork is roasting, make the pear sauce. Heat the butter in a pan and sizzle the pear and fennel seeds together until they start to brown. Add the perry or cider and sugar. Bubble down until the liquid is reduced, sticky and caramelized, and the pear is very tender. Use a potato masher to mash the pear into a rough purée. Serve the sauce alongside the pork with your favourite side dishes.

Per serving: 530 kcalories, protein 41.2g, carbohydrate 16.8g, fat 32.8g, saturated fat 12.4g, fibre 2.2, sugar 15.9g, salt 0.32g

■ We've collected a range of side dishes for you to try. Make them when the ingredients are in season so you can buy them at their best price.

Spinach and green bean salad

This is quick and simple to do. Prepare the beans and dressing ahead, then toss together just before serving. This will make lots, so have your largest bowl to hand.

Serves 8 ■ prep 10 mins

2 × 250g packs fine green beans, stalk ends trimmed
3 tbsp olive oil
juice 1 lemon
180g bag baby leaf spinach salad

1 Bring a pan of water to the boil. Fill a large bowl with very cold, ideally iced water. Plunge the beans into the boiling water for 1–2 mins until just softened. Drain from the pan with a slotted spoon and drop straight into the iced water.

2 In a small bowl, mix the olive oil and lemon juice, and season with salt and freshly ground black pepper. Mix the beans and spinach in a large serving bowl. Toss the salad with the dressing and serve immediately.

Per serving: 58 kcalories, protein 2g, carbohydrate 2g, fat 5g, saturated fat 1g, fibre 2g, added sugar none, salt 0.08g

Melting cheese courgettes

This super-healthy side dish is great with grilled chicken or fish.

1 Heat olive oil in a large non-stick frying pan or griddle pan. Rub the courgettes in the oil, season then fry or griddle for 3–5 mins on each side until softened and golden.

2 Transfer to a serving bowl, then toss with the parmesan, lemon zest and plenty of black pepper. Drizzle with extra olive oil to serve, if you like.

Per serving: 100 kcalories, protein 5g, carbohydrate 2g, fat 8g, saturated fat 2g, fibre 1g, sugar 2g, salt 0.16g

TIP You can easily make the courgettes into a bake. Put the griddled courgettes into a medium baking dish and toss with the remaining ingredients, plus 4 tbsp crème fraîche. Top with a little more parmesan and, when ready to serve, grill or bake until softened and the sauce is bubbling.

Serves 2 ▪ prep 5 mins ▪ cook 10 mins

1 tbsp olive oil, plus extra to drizzle (optional)
200g/8oz baby courgettes, halved lengthways (or 4 ordinary courgettes, sliced thickly)
handful finely grated parmesan
zest 1 lemon

Lemon-roasted new potatoes

An easy idea for roast potatoes with a twist.

Serves 2 ▪ prep 2 mins
▪ cook 35 mins

450g/1lb new potatoes
zest 1 lemon
1 tbsp olive oil

1   Heat oven to 200C/fan 180C/gas 6. Tip the potatoes into a large pan of boiling water, bring to the boil, then cook for 5 mins. Drain, tip the potatoes back into the pan and shake well to rough up the edges a little.

2   Tip on to a baking sheet, toss with the lemon zest, oil and some sea salt, then roast for 30 mins until golden and crisp.

Per serving: 207 kcalories, protein 4g, carbohydrate 36g, fat 6g, saturated fat 1g, fibre 2g, sugar 3g, salt 0.06g

Saffron wild rice

Fragrant saffron with a nutty-flavoured scattering of black wild rice and basmati grains. Go easy on the saffron as a little goes a long way — overdo it and the flavour takes over.

1 Tip the rice into a microwave-proof bowl. Sprinkle over the saffron and pour over the hot stock. Cover with cling film, then pierce it a couple of times. Microwave for 6 mins on High, then 6–8 mins on Medium until the rice is tender.

Per serving: 256 kcalories, protein 8g, carbohydrate 58g, fat 1g, saturated fat none, fibre none, added sugar none, salt 0.50g

TIP If you don't have a microwave, simply follow the pack instructions for conventional boiling times.

Serves 4 ▪ prep 2 mins
▪ cook 6–8 mins

300g/10oz basmati and wild rice
good pinch of saffron
600ml/1pint vegetable stock

Winter root mash

You only need a spoonful of this as it is so divinely rich with cream. Make it a day ahead, so all you have to do before your guests arrive is reheat it in the oven.

1 Cook the parsnips and swede in a pan of salted water, covered, for about 20 mins until tender. Drain well, then mash them using a masher or food processor until smooth but still with a bit of texture. Stir in the soured cream, horseradish and thyme, and season. Spoon into a buttered shallow ovenproof dish and put to one side.

2 To make the topping, melt the butter in a frying pan and cook the onion for 5–6 mins, until golden. Mix in the breadcrumbs and stir until browned, then season. Spoon the mixture over the mash. Scatter over the parmesan. The dish can be made ahead to this point, kept covered in the fridge for up to a day or frozen for a month.

3 Heat oven to 190C/fan 170C/gas 5. Bake the mash for 25–30 mins. If cooking from chilled, bake for 35–40 mins or bake for 1½–1¾ hours if cooking from frozen (cover with foil, then remove it for the last 10 mins) – until golden and crisp on top. Serve scattered with a few more thyme sprigs and leaves.

Per serving (10): 158 kcalories, protein 4g, carbohydrate 17g, fat 9g, saturated fat 5g, fibre 5g, added sugar none, salt 0.57g

Serves 10 ■ prep 50–60 mins ■ cook 25–40 mins

650g/1lb 7oz parsnips, chopped into even-sized chunks
650g/1lb 7oz swede, chopped into same size chunks as parsnips
142ml pot soured cream
1 rounded tbsp hot horseradish
2 tbsp fresh thyme leaves, plus extra sprigs and leaves for scattering
butter for greasing
for the butter topping
50g/2oz butter
1 small onion, finely chopped
50g/2oz white breadcrumbs (about 4 slices)
25g/1oz parmesan, coarsely grated

Spiced red cabbage

Make in advance for a stress-free meal.

1 Peel off the outer leaves of the cabbage, cut into quarters and slice out the core, then thinly slice the cabbage.

2 Heat the butter in a large pan, then tip in the onions and gently fry until softened, about 5 mins. Add the orange zest to the pan along with the cinnamon stick, then cook for 1 min more. Add the shredded cabbage, then pour over the port, red wine vinegar, orange juice and 150ml of water. Bring to the boil, reduce the heat to a simmer, cover the pan and cook for 45 mins–1 hour until the cabbage is softened.

Per serving: 82 kcalories, protein 2g, carbohydrate 10g, fat 3g, saturated fat 2g, fibre 4g, sugar 9g, salt 0.08g

Serves 8 ■ prep 25 mins ■ cook 1 hour

1 large red cabbage (about 1kg/2lb 4oz)
25g/1oz butter
2 red onions, finely chopped
zest and juice 1 orange
1 cinnamon stick
150ml/¼ pint port
1 tbsp red wine vinegar

■ Round off your weekend feast with these crowd-pleasing puds that won't break the bank.

Chocolate pecan fondants ❄

These indulgent 'afters' are great to freeze, so why not make an extra batch?

Makes 4 ■ prep 20 mins ■ cook 15–20 mins

100g/4oz butter, plus extra for greasing
cocoa powder, for dusting
300g/10oz plain chocolate (50% cocoa solids is fine), chopped into chunks
2 eggs, beaten
4 tbsp plain flour
4 tbsp pecan nuts, toasted and chopped very finely
2 tbsp golden caster sugar

1   Heat oven to 220C/fan 200C/gas 7. Butter four 200ml individual pudding basins, then dust generously with cocoa powder. Melt the chocolate with the butter in a bowl over simmering water or in a microwave and stir until smooth. Gradually stir in the eggs, then the flour, nuts, sugar and a pinch of salt, and beat gently until everything is combined but still runny.

2   Divide the mixture among the pudding basins. These can now be chilled for up to a day ahead. Bake for 15 mins (or 18 mins if chilled). Turn out onto small plates and serve with ice cream. The fondants should be cooked on the outside and molten in the middle.

Per serving: 825 kcalories, protein 11.9g, carbohydrate 55.5g, fat 63.2g, saturated fat 30.9g, fibre 5.5g, sugar 29.9g, salt 0.53g

Classic vanilla ice cream ❄

Good vanilla ice cream is smooth and creamy. This recipe makes about 500g/1lb 2oz – the size of the average luxury-brand tub.

1 Put a container in the freezer. Split the vanilla pod lengthways, scrape out the seeds with the point of the knife and tip into a pan with the milk, cream and pod. Bring to the boil, then remove from the heat and leave to infuse for at least 20 mins. For the best flavour, make a few hours beforehand and leave to go cold.

2 In a large bowl, whisk the sugar and egg yolks together for a few mins until they turn pale and fluffy. Put the vanilla cream back on the heat until it's just about to boil, then carefully sieve the liquid on to the yolks, beating with the whisk until completely mixed.

3 Sit a small bowl in a larger bowl of iced water. Pour the custard back into the pan and cook on the lowest heat, stirring slowly and continuously, making sure the spoon touches the bottom of the pan, for about 10 mins until thickened. Strain the custard into the smaller bowl sitting in the iced water and leave to cool, then churn until scoopable with an ice-cream machine, a hand blender or by hand (see Know-how). Transfer to the cold container and freeze.

Per serving: 396 kcalories, protein 5g, carbohydrate 21g, fat 33g, saturated fat 18g, fibre none, sugar 21g, salt none.

Serves 6 ■ prep 10 mins, plus cooling, churning and freezing ■ cook 20 mins

1 plump vanilla pod
300ml/½ pint full-fat milk
300ml/½ pint double cream
100g/4oz golden caster sugar
4 egg yolks

KNOW-HOW Homemade ice cream is best served within a week of being made, but will still be fine for up to a month. If frozen solid, remove the ice cream from the freezer and leave it to defrost in the fridge for an hour before serving.

Churning methods
Once you have made your custard base, there are three different methods for turning it into ice cream.

Machine The easiest way to achieve the velvety texture you get in a shop-bought ice cream is with an ice-cream machine. Some require the bowl to be pre-frozen; others you can just switch on and go. Whichever machine you use, once set up, you simply pour in the cooled custard and churn the custard until it's frozen, then transfer to a chilled container.
Hand Very good ice cream can be made without a machine. Put your cooled mix in a metal bowl in the freezer and when it becomes slushy, whisk it hard. Place back in the freezer and repeat the process two more times, then leave to freeze until scoopable. Finally, transfer to a smaller container, adding chunks or ripples if you want.
Hand blender You can also use a hand blender. Place the chilled custard in a plastic jug or tall freezer-proof container and put in the freezer. When it's slushy, blitz it with a hand blender. Repeat the process two more times and leave to freeze until scoopable.

Raspberry ripple Pavlova

Here pavlova is filled with spoonfuls of semi-freddo (half-frozen, soft-scoop ice cream) instead of whipped cream.

Serves 6 ■ **prep 30–35 mins, plus cooling and freezing**
■ **cook 1¼–1½ hours**

250g/9oz raspberries
50g/2oz icing sugar
284ml pot double cream
250g pot mascarpone
3 large egg whites, at room
   temperature
175g/6oz caster sugar
1 tsp cornflour
handful unsalted pistachio nuts,
   chopped

1   Make the semi-freddo. Push 140g of the raspberries through a sieve, leaving behind the seeds. Stir in 25g of the icing sugar. Whip the cream until like thick custard. Whisk in the mascarpone until the mix thickens, then stir in the remaining icing sugar.

2   Drop spoonfuls of the cream mix into a deep, oblong plastic container, and fill in with a drizzle of sieved raspberries. Do not stir. Add another layer of cream and raspberries. Gently smooth the surface and press down lightly, then freeze for 2–2½ hours until half frozen.

3   Heat oven to 140C/fan 120C/gas 1. Line a large baking sheet with non-stick baking parchment. Draw a 20–22cm circle on the paper. In a large, clean bowl, whisk the egg whites until stiff peaks form. Slowly whisk in the caster sugar until thick and glossy. Beat in the cornflour. Pile the meringue in soft folds on to the circle on the baking parchment. Scatter over the pistachios. Bake for 1¼–1½ hours until crisp on the outside and dry underneath. Cool then gently peel off the paper.

4   Remove the semi-freddo from the freezer and pile in big spoonfuls on the pavlova. Finish off with a scattering of the remaining raspberries.

Per serving: 593 kcalories, protein 5g, carbohydrate 46g, fat 44g, saturated fat 27g, fibre 1g, added sugar 38g, salt 0.59g

Summer pudding

A classic thrifty pud. When berries are in season and plentiful, it is cheap to make and tastes fantastic.

1 Wash the fruit and gently dry on kitchen paper – keep the strawberries separate. Put the sugar and 3 tbsp of water into a large pan. Gently heat until the sugar dissolves – stir a few times. Bring to the boil for 1 min, then tip in the fruit (not strawberries). Cook for 3 mins over a low heat, stirring 2–3 times. The fruit will be softened, mostly intact and surrounded by dark red juice. Put a sieve over a bowl and tip in the fruit to drain the juice. Reserve the juice for later.

2 Line a 1.25-litre pudding basin with cling film (this will help you to turn out the pudding later). Overlap two pieces in the middle of the bowl as it's easier than trying to get one sheet to stick to all of the curves. Let the edges overhang by about 15cm. Cut the crusts off the bread. Cut four slices of bread in half, a little on an angle, to give two lopsided rectangles per slice. Cut two slices into four triangles each and leave the final slice whole.

3 Dip the whole slice of bread into the strained juice for a few secs just to coat. Push this into the bottom of the basin. Now dip the wonky rectangular pieces in the juice one at a time and press around the basin's sides so that they fit together neatly, alternately placing wide and narrow ends up. If you can't quite fit the last piece of bread in, it doesn't matter, just trim to fit, dip in the juice and slot in. Now spoon in the softened strained fruit, adding the strawberries here and there as you go.

4 Dip the bread triangles in juice and place on top – trim off the overhang with scissors. Keep any leftover juice for later. Bring the cling film up and loosely seal. Put a side plate on top and weight down with cans. Chill for 6 hours or overnight. To serve, open out the cling film then put a serving plate upside-down on top and flip over. Serve with leftover juice, any extra berries and cream.

Per serving: 248 kcalories, protein 6g, carbohydrate 57g, fat 1g, saturated fat none, fibre 9g, added sugar 43g, salt 0.45g

Serves 8 ■ prep 20 mins, plus chilling ■ cook 10 mins

1.25kg/2lb 12oz mixed berries and currants (we used 300g/10oz strawberries, quartered, 250g/9oz blackberries, 100g/4oz each blackcurrants and redcurrants, 500g/1lb 2oz raspberries)
175g/6oz golden caster sugar
7 slices from a square medium-cut white sliced loaf, day-old is best
double cream, to serve

Mango and cardamom syllabub

These delicious fruity desserts are perfect for entertaining as they can be made just before your guests arrive.

Makes 8 ▪ prep 25 mins

4 large mangoes, peeled and
   stoned, 2 finely chopped
10 green cardamom pods,
   deseeded
zest and juice 2 limes
85g/3oz icing sugar
4 tbsp brandy
568ml pot double cream
4 meringue nests, lightly crushed
fresh mint sprigs, to serve

1   Put the flesh of the 2 unchopped mangoes in a food processor and blend to a purée. Stir in almost all the finely chopped flesh of the other 2 mangoes, then spoon into the base of eight glasses. Grind the cardamom seeds to a powder, then put in a bowl with the lime zest and juice, icing sugar and brandy. Stir well, then tip in the cream and whip until it holds its shape. Gently fold in the crushed meringue.

2   Spoon the cream mixture on top of the mango purée, then spoon the remaining chopped mango on top. This dessert can be made 1 hour ahead. Serve decorated with mint sprigs.

Per syllabub: 525 kcalories, protein 2.5g, carbohydrate 40.7g, fat 38.5g, saturated fat 21.4g, fibre 3.9g, sugar 40g, salt 0.07g

TIP Don't make these too far in advance – the meringue will start to dissolve. If you would rather make the syllabubs a day ahead, make them without the meringue, but serve the meringues whole on the side to eat separately. It's also an easy pudding to halve, if you have fewer guests.

Roast pears in red wine

A traditional autumn dessert that's so easy to make.

Serves 6 ∎ prep 10 mins
∎ cook 1 hour 10 mins

6–8 Comice pears
250ml/9fl oz red wine
50g/2oz butter
100g/4oz demerara sugar
2 cinnamon sticks, broken in half
2 star anise

1 Heat oven to 200C/fan 180C/gas 6. Cut a small slice off the bottom of each pear so they sit up. Put the pears into an ovenproof casserole dish and pour over the wine. Cut the butter into cubes and press a cube on to the top of each pear. Sprinkle over the sugar, scatter around the cinnamon and star anise. Cover with a lid or foil, then bake in the oven for 30 mins.

2 Remove the pears from the oven, baste them well in their juices then return to the oven, uncovered, for 40 mins, basting occasionally, until the pears are soft and wrinkled. The pears can be prepared up to this point up to 2 days ahead and reheated in a low oven (150C/fan 130C/gas 6). Serve the pears warm with the juices and a spoonful of mascarpone.

Per serving: 193 kcalories, protein 0.6g, carbohydrate 30.9g, fat 6.8g, saturated fat 4.3g, fibre 2.7g, sugar 30.9g, salt 0.15g.

Deep-filled apple pie ❄

Autumn calls for comfort food, and this pie does it best. Serve with custard, ice cream or cream.

Serves 8 ■ prep 30 mins ■ cook 40 mins

200g/8oz sultanas
5 tbsp brandy
plain flour, for dusting
750g (2 x 375g packs) all-butter
    shortcrust pastry
5 medium Bramley apples, peeled,
    cored and finely sliced
140g/5oz golden caster sugar
½ tsp each ground cinnamon,
    nutmeg and allspice
1 egg, beaten with a splash of milk

1 Heat oven to 200C/fan 180C/gas 6. Tip the sultanas into a bowl with the brandy, microwave on High for a few secs until warm and plump, then set aside. Dust a work surface with flour. If the pastry is in two blocks, squish it together, then cut off a third and set aside. Roll out the rest of the pastry into a large circle, about the thickness of a £1 coin. Use it to line a 23cm shallow springform cake tin, making sure that it overhangs the rim all the way round. Put in the fridge.

2 Tip the apples into the bowl with the sultanas, all but 2 tbsp of the sugar and the spices. Toss everything well to coat the apple. Roll out the rest of the pastry, then cut into a circle, using the base of the tin as a guide. Using your fingers, arrange the apple slices in the cake tin. Cover the apples with the circle of pastry and tuck down the sides. Fold back and pinch the overhang to seal. Brush the top generously with egg, then make two slits in the top with a knife and scatter over the remaining sugar. The pie can be wrapped and frozen at this point.

3 Bake for 30-35 mins until golden. Leave to cool in the tin for 1 hour, until the bottom is cool enough to touch. Run a knife around the pie edge, then spring open the tin and remove the pie. Serve sliced while still warm.

Per serving: 646 kcalories, protein 8g, carbohydrate 93g, fat 27g, saturated fat 11g, fibre 4g, sugar 48g, salt 1g

Sponge pudding

This pud has half the fat of the classic recipe, but all the flavour.

Serves 6 ▪ prep 20 mins
▪ cook 1¼ hours

1 large eating apple, cut into
    quarters
140g/5oz fresh or frozen
    blackberries or raspberries
50g/2oz golden caster sugar, plus
    2 tbsp
140g/5oz plain flour
1½ tsp baking powder
50g/2oz light muscovado sugar
85g/3oz butter, softened
2 eggs
2 tbsp milk
zest 1 orange

1 Very lightly butter a 1-litre pudding basin. Heat oven to 180C/ fan 160C/gas 4. Coarsely grate one of the apple quarters and thinly slice the rest. Combine the sliced apple and blackberries or raspberries, toss with the 2 tbsp of caster sugar and spoon half into the bottom of the basin.

2 Mix together the flour and baking powder. Beat both the sugars and butter together in a large bowl with a handheld electric mixer until light and creamy. Break in 1 egg and beat well, then beat in the second egg (the mixture will look curdled). Sift half the flour mixture over the sponge mixture and fold in gently. Carefully stir in half the milk, then repeat with the rest of the flour and milk, followed by the orange zest and reserved grated apple.

3 Spoon two-thirds of the sponge mixture over the fruit mix in the basin and level off. Spread the rest of the fruit on top, followed by the remaining sponge mix. Put the basin in a small roasting tin half-filled with water. Bake for 1½ hours (lay foil over the top for the last 15 mins if it is browning too quickly) until a skewer inserted into the middle comes out clean.

4 Loosen the pudding from the sides of the basin with a round-bladed knife and carefully invert on to a serving plate. Serve with custard poured over the top or alongside.

Per serving: 320 kcalories, protein 5.3g, carbohydrate 45.3g, fat 14.3g, saturated fat 8.1g, fibre 1.9, sugar 27.1g, salt 0.68g.

Bread and butter pudding

Delicious, creamy, pure comfort food. This is an enduring favourite.

1　Heat oven to 140C/fan 120C/gas 1. Stir the custard together with the milk. Trim the crusts from the bread, cut into triangles, then place in a large bowl with the raisins or dried cherries. Pour over the custard mixture, then carefully stir everything together so all the pieces of bread are coated. Lightly grease a small ovenproof dish with butter, then spoon in the mixture.

2　Cook for 30–35 mins until there is just a slight wobble in the centre of the custard. Sprinkle over the sugar to cover the surface, then pop under a hot grill for 1–2 mins until the sugar starts to melt and caramelize.

Per serving: 363 kcalories, protein 7g, carbohydrate 64g, fat 11g, saturated fat 7g, fibre 1g, sugar 47g, salt 0.57g

Serves 4 ▪ prep 5 mins ▪ cook 35–40 mins

568ml pot fresh custard
150ml/¼ pint full-fat milk
140g/5oz white bread
50g/2oz raisins or dried cherries
butter, for greasing
5–7 tbsp caster sugar

Baking

- Make some time for baking over the weekend — it's so satisfying and relaxing, and the house will smell lovely!

Easy white bread ❄

This recipe also works well in a breadmaker, if you have one. Just add all the ingredients to the machine and follow the manufacturer's instructions.

1   Mix the flour, salt and yeast in a large bowl. Make a well in the centre, then add the oil and water, and mix well. If the dough seems a little stiff, add a further 1—2 tbsp of water, mix well then tip on to a lightly floured work surface and knead. Once the dough is satin-smooth, put it in a lightly oiled bowl. Leave to rise for 1 hour until doubled in size or put in the fridge overnight.

2   Line a baking sheet with non-stick baking parchment. Knock back the dough, then gently mould into a ball. Place it on the baking parchment to prove for a further hour until doubled in size.

3   Heat oven to 220C/fan 200C/gas 7. Dust the loaf with flour and cut a cross about 6cm long into the top of the loaf with a sharp knife. Bake for 25—30 mins until golden brown and the loaf sounds hollow when tapped underneath. Cool on a wire rack.

Per serving: 204 kcalories, protein 6g, carbohydrate 38g, fat 4g, saturated fat 1g, fibre 2g, added sugar none, salt 1g

KNOW-HOW A dough's first rising can be done in the fridge overnight. This slows down the time it takes to rise to double its size, giving it a deeper flavour. It's also a great timesaver if you want to make bread regularly, as you can start it the night before, then finish it off the next day.

Makes 1 loaf ■ prep 20 mins, plus 2 hours proving ■ cook 25—30 mins

500g/1lb 2oz strong white flour, plus extra for dusting
2 tsp salt
7g sachet fast-action yeast
3 tbsp olive oil, plus extra for oiling
300ml/½ pint water, at room temperature

Potato focaccia Pugliese ❄

Basic bread dough can be made into something special by adding potatoes and rosemary, as in this classic Italian recipe. Perfect for a light lunch, served with a salad.

Serves 8 ■ prep 25 mins, plus 2 hours proving ■ cook 30 mins

500g/1lb 2oz strong white flour, plus extra for dusting
2 tsp salt, plus rock salt for sprinkling (optional)
7g sachet fast-action yeast
splash of olive oil, plus extra for oiling and drizzling
300ml/½ pint water, at room temperature
400g/14oz new potatoes (about 8–10), sliced to the thickness of a £1 coin
2 fresh rosemary sprigs

1 Mix the flour, salt and yeast in a large bowl. Make a well in the centre, add the oil and water, and mix well. If the dough seems a little stiff, add a further 1–2 tbsp of water, mix again, then put on a lightly floured work surface and knead well. Put the dough in a lightly oiled bowl. Leave to rise for 1 hour until doubled in size.

2 Remove the dough from the bowl, knock back, then spread out with your hands on to a large, oiled 20x30cm baking tray. Brush with olive oil and make deep indentations with your fingers. Layer the potatoes and rosemary leaves over the top, and drizzle with a little more oil. Leave to prove for 1 hour until doubled in size.

3 Heat oven to 230C/fan 210C/gas 8. Sprinkle the dough with a little rock salt, if you like. Bake the bread for 30 mins until it is golden and sounds hollow when tapped underneath, and the potatoes are tender. Drizzle the loaf with more olive oil, if you like, and, when cooled, serve on the tray.

Per serving: 266 kcalories, protein 8g, carbohydrate 55g, fat 3g, saturated fat none, fibre 2g, added sugar none, salt 1.3g

Pumpkin and ginger teabread ❄

A good cake is always worth making to enjoy at the weekend; don't tell anyone there's pumpkin in it and watch them try to guess what gives it such an interesting taste and texture.

1 Heat oven to 180C/fan 160C/gas 4. Butter and line the base and two long sides of a 1.5kg loaf tin with a strip of non-stick baking paper.

2 Mix the butter, honey and egg, and stir in the pumpkin or squash. Then mix in the sugar, flour and ginger.

3 Pour into the prepared tin and sprinkle the top with the demerara sugar. Bake for 50–60 mins, until risen and golden brown. Leave in the tin for 5 mins, then turn out and cool on a wire rack. Serve thickly sliced and buttered.

Per slice: 351 kcalories, protein 4g, carbohydrate 52g, fat 15g, saturated fat 9g, fibre 1g, added sugar 24g, salt 0.69g

Cuts into 10 slices
- **prep 25–30 mins**
- **cook 50–60 mins**

175g/6oz butter, melted, plus extra for greasing
140g/5oz clear honey
1 large egg, beaten
250g/9oz pumpkin or butternut squash, peeled, deseeded and coarsely grated (about 500g/1lb 2oz before peeling and deseeding)
100g/4oz light muscovado sugar
350g/12oz self-raising flour
1 tbsp ground ginger
2 tbsp demerara sugar

Banana cake

This cake is so good, not just for its great flavour but also because it's such a handy way to use up over-ripe bananas.

1   Heat oven to 180C/fan 160C/gas 4, and line the base and sides of a deep 20cm loose-bottomed cake tin with non-stick baking parchment. For the crumble topping, stir together 2 tbsp each of the sugar, flour and chopped pecans. Add the butter, cut into a few pieces and rub together until you have sticky crumbs then set aside.

2   Break up the whole eggs with a fork, then mix with the mashed banana, oil and milk until all the wet ingredients are well combined. In a separate, large bowl tip in the remaining sugar, flour and pecans, and briefly stir in the cinnamon and baking powder. Whisk the egg whites until just stiff.

3   Tip the oily banana mixture into the bowl of dry ingredients and quickly stir in until you have a smooth, lump-free mix. Finally using a large metal spoon or spatula gently fold in the egg whites, then carefully pour the mixture into the prepared tin. Scatter over the crumble topping and bake for 1 hour, until a skewer inserted into the middle comes out clean. Check the cake with 15 mins to go, if the surface is browning too quickly cover with another piece of baking parchment. Once the cake is ready, leave it in the tin for 5 mins, then remove from the tin and finish cooling on a wire rack.

Per serving (8): 595 kcalories, protein 8.2g, carbohydrate 70.2g, fat 33.2g, saturated fat 4.9g, fibre 2.3g, sugar 45g, salt 0.62g

Cuts into 8-10 slices ▪ prep 20 mins ▪ cook 1 hour

250g/9oz golden caster sugar
250g/9oz self-raising flour
140g/5oz pecans, roughly chopped
1 tbsp butter
2 eggs, plus 2 egg whites
3 large ripe bananas, or 4 small, mashed
150ml/¼ pint sunflower oil
100ml/3½fl oz milk
1 tsp ground cinnamon
1 tsp baking powder

Stocks

■ It's really easy to make a good homemade stock, especially as you've probably got all the ingredients to hand. When you have a bit of time, try one of these three basic stocks — they all freeze beautifully.

Vegetable stock ❄

You can add any veg trimmings to this, such as broccoli, fennel or tomato. For a fuller-flavoured stock, use the water from the steamer after cooking vegetables instead of tap water.

Makes about 600ml/1 pint
■ **prep 5 mins**
■ **cook 30–40 mins**

2 celery sticks, roughly chopped, (use the leaves too, if you have them)
2 large carrots, roughly chopped
1 large onion or 2 small, chopped
1–2 leeks, roughly chopped
1 tbsp black peppercorns, about 12–14
2 bay leaves
small handful fresh parsley stalks

1 Put all the ingredients into a pan, with a pinch of salt and cover with 850ml water. Put a lid on the pan, bring to the boil and simmer briskly for 30–40 mins.

2 Strain to reserve the liquid, discarding the veg, and cool, if not using straight away. To freeze, carry on boiling to reduce the stock down further, then decant into freezer bags or containers, ice-cube trays work well too. Remember to dilute the stock with boiling water before using.

Chicken stock ❄

Homemade chicken stock tastes so much better than shop-bought.

1 Put all the ingredients into a pan, with a pinch of salt. Cover with 1 litre of water then put the lid on the pan. Bring to the boil, simmer for 1¼ hours – the liquid will reduce by about half. You may need to skim the surface as it simmers to remove any scum.

2 Strain the stock, discarding the chicken and veg. Cool, if not using straight away. You can freeze the stock at this stage, if the chicken bones haven't been cooked and frozen before.

TIP If you've bought a chicken without giblets, you can use the wings and tips; if you want to make a bigger batch, you can use the carcass of the chicken. This works as well with turkey too.

Makes about 600ml/1 pint
- **prep 10 mins**
- **cook 1¼hours-1½hours**

giblets from 1 chicken
1 stick celery, halved (use the leaves too, if you have them)
2 large carrots, halved
1 onion, chopped
2 leeks, roughly chopped
1 tbsp peppercorns, about 12–14
2 bay leaves
small handful fresh parsley stalks
2 fresh sprigs rosemary or thyme, (optional)

Fish stock ❄

A light, clear fish stock is a good base for all kinds of soups, risottos and fish dishes. You can use prawn shells and fish bone, instead of the fish trimmings, if you want a stronger-tasting stock.

1 Put all the ingredients into a pan, season with salt and pepper then cover with 700ml of water. Bring to the boil, and simmer for 30 mins, skim the surface once or twice to remove any scum.

2 Strain, discarding all the other ingredients. Cool, if not using straight away. You can freeze the stock at this stage, if the fish trimmings or shellfish bones haven't been frozen before.

Makes about 600ml/1 pint
- **prep 5 mins**
- **cook 30-40 mins**

450g/1lb fish bits, trimmings are good, rinsed
1 small glass white wine, dry is best
1 leek, thickly chopped
2 celery sticks or 1 fennel bulb, roughly chopped
1 carrot
½ tbsp black peppercorns
small handful fresh parsley stalks
1 large or 2 small bay leaves

chapter 6

The meal planners

The following meal planners are suggestions, but there are no hard and fast rules, so tweak them to suit your schedule. If you've got a hectic weekend and know you won't get a minute to do much cooking, then dip into the weekday suppers or budget family dinners chapters to make something from there. If you haven't had time to shop, simply whip up a meal with ingredients already stored in your cupboard or freezer using a recipe from chapter 4. The key to thrifty cooking is planning.

This chapter is here to help you to plan meals and draw up shopping lists. We've chosen some dishes for the weekend that take a little more time to cook as well as quicker ones for the weekdays. We've also given you something from each chapter to give you a wide range of meals each week.

As well as entertaining menus and batch cooking for the weekend, there are cheap family dinners that you can make in a flash, weekday suppers that will form part of a meal the next day and then a meal that you can assemble from your well-stocked freezer, storecupboard and fridge. Then, when you're tired or just want a night off, there's always the batch meal that you made at the weekend, ready in the freezer. Each recipe is colour-coded and includes the recipe page number, so you can see what type of recipe it is and where to find it.

We've thought about how to spread the cost of shopping too. There are meals that include meat, some with fish, others that use tinned or frozen cheaper ingredients and a number that are packed full of veg.

Why not try a couple each month, so that you don't have to think of new ideas all the time? There are checklists after each meal planner with tips on how to make them more flexible.

plan 1		
SATURDAY	**Lamb shanks with chickpeas, Classic vanilla ice cream** (pages 178 and 191)	
SUNDAY	**Italian-style beef** (page 40)	
MONDAY	**Oven-baked pepper risotto** (page 54)	
TUESDAY	**Risotto cakes** (page 54)	
WEDNESDAY	**Easy noodles** (page 109)	
THURSDAY	**Tuna melt potato wedges** (page 124)	
FRIDAY	**Italian-style beef** (page 40)	

Checklist

■ Lamb shanks have rocketed in price as they've become a fashionable cut, but are ideal for a casual meal with friends. Choose medium-size ones to keep down the cost; there will still be plenty for everyone.

■ Serve the ice cream with hot chocolate sauce or a shot of espresso coffee poured over.

■ The risotto cakes use leftover rice. Make sure you chill it quickly after cooking.

■ Make a double quantity of the beef stew and freeze half so that there's enough for later in the week. Take Friday's portion out on Thursday evening and defrost in the fridge.

plan 2		
SATURDAY	**Tomato tarte Tatin, Steamed mussels** (pages 113 and 160)	
SUNDAY	**Chilli con carne** (page 11)	
MONDAY	**Fragrant roast chicken** (page 75)	
TUESDAY	**No-cook chicken couscous** (page 76)	
WEDNESDAY	**Chilli con carne** (page 11)	
THURSDAY	**20-minute seafood spaghetti** (page 105)	
FRIDAY	**Pizza Margherita** (page 128)	

Checklist

■ Serving two starters is a great cheap meal for a weekend lunch or casual supper.

■ Make double of the chilli and pop half in the freezer. It reheats straight from frozen so you can swap meals around and have it later in the week, if you like.

■ Get into the weekend with a pizza night. Everyone can choose their favourite toppings from fridge leftovers.

Checklist

■ Buy a pumpkin instead of butternut squash for the cassoulet. If you buy enough for the teabread as well, you can use any leftovers to make a lunchtime salad.

■ Make double of the cassoulet and freeze half. Take it out of the freezer in the morning, and it will be ready to bake by the evening.

■ Scrambled eggs make a good speedy supper when everyone may need feeding at different times.

SATURDAY	**Sausage and lentil simmer, Pumpkin teabread** (pages 168 and 203)	
SUNDAY	**Roast vegetable cassoulet** (page 24)	
MONDAY	**Quick roast lamb** (page 102)	
TUESDAY	**Scrambled egg muffin** (page 125)	
WEDNESDAY	**Good-for-you bolognese** (page 58)	
THURSDAY	**Shepherd's pie jackets** (page 58)	
FRIDAY	**Roast vegetable cassoulet** (page 24)	

Checklist

■ Soufflés and braised oxtail make a smart but filling dinner that probably doesn't need a pudding, though the apple pie (page 196) would go well, if you wanted to make one.

■ Chicken casserole is a great freezer stand-by, so make double and freeze half for later. Take it out of the freezer on Thursday evening to defrost in the fridge overnight.

■ Make extra mash the day before for the fish cakes (you can even make the fish cakes the same night and leave them in the fridge to chill until ready to cook).

SATURDAY	**Goat's cheese soufflés, Oxtail with basil dumplings** (page 159 and 176)	
SUNDAY	**Chicken casserole with red wine, ham and peppers** (page 30)	
MONDAY	**Best-ever macaroni cheese** (page 141)	
TUESDAY	**Oriental bangers and mash** (page 68)	
WEDNESDAY	**Salmon and pea fishcakes** (page 69)	
THURSDAY	**Baked haddock risotto and cabbage** (page 95)	
FRIDAY	**Chicken casserole with red wine, ham and peppers** (page 30)	

SATURDAY	**Fish pie** (page 39)
SUNDAY	**Roast pork with pear, Chocolate pecan fondants** (pages 182 and 190)
MONDAY	**Mixed bean goulash** (page 138)
TUESDAY	**Kale pasta with chilli and anchovy** (page 66)
WEDNESDAY	**Hot pasta salad** (page 67)
THURSDAY	**Sticky chicken with mango couscous** (page 88)
FRIDAY	**Fish pie** (page 39)

Checklist

■   This is a good menu for the early months of the year, when seasonal veg is scarce.

■   The weekend is a great time to make a fish pie, especially if your local market has a good fish stall.

■   For the Hot pasta salad, you could omit the rocket and use any leftover herbs from the fish pie instead.

■   Take the fish pie out the night before you want to serve it. Defrost it in the fridge.

SATURDAY	**Goat's cheese soufflés, Braised pork with prunes** (pages 159 and 175)
SUNDAY	**Roast vegetable cassoulet** (page 24)
MONDAY	**Warm stilton salad** (page 64)
TUESDAY	**Creamy mushroom spaghetti** (page 64)
WEDNESDAY	**Spiced carrot and lentil soup** (page 113)
THURSDAY	**Roast vegetable cassoulet** (page 24)
FRIDAY	**Toad-in-the-hole with red onions and thyme batter** (page 137)

Checklist

■   If you serve a cheeseboard for a dinner party at the week-end, then buy extra stilton to use it in the meals during the week.

■   Vary the vegetables in the cassoulet each time you make it, depending what's on offer. Make double for the meal in the week. Freeze and take it out of the freezer on Thursday morning.

■   Any leftover soup makes a good lunch the next day.

■   A storecupboard meal can still be hearty and filling, like this toad-in-the-hole, which just requires sausages in the freezer.

Checklist

■ Brisket is a fantastically cost-effective cut, and braising it in beer will tenderize it beautifully.

■ The individual shepherd's pies are ideal for the freezer, but you can make a big one for the weekend meal.

plan 7

SATURDAY	Pot-roasted brisket in beer, Deep-filled apple pie (pages 181 and 196)
SUNDAY	Veggie shepherd's pie with sweet potato mash (page 15)
MONDAY	Cauliflower cheese (page 59)
TUESDAY	Cheesy gammon grills (page 59)
WEDNESDAY	Spiced sweet potato salad with crisp noodles (page 90)
THURSDAY	Crab and lemon linguine (page 145)
FRIDAY	Veggie shepherd's pie with sweet potato mash (page 115)

Checklist

■ If you're at the fishmongers for mussels, pick up enough smoked haddock to make a filling soup for in the week.

■ You can freeze the soup, and, when ready to use, defrost it in the fridge.

■ Egg and chips are the perfect pairing for a comforting but quick midweek meal.

plan 8

SATURDAY	Steamed mussels, Slow-cooked lamb, Apple pie (pages 160, 173 and 196)
SUNDAY	Smoked haddock chowder (page 47)
MONDAY	One-pot mushroom and potato curry (page 51)
TUESDAY	Fast-fix fried rice (page 51)
WEDNESDAY	Healthy egg and chips (page 110)
THURSDAY	10-minute tortellini (page 140)
FRIDAY	Smoked haddock chowder (page 47)

plan 9

SATURDAY	**Five-a-day tagine** (page 18)
SUNDAY	**Greek roast lamb, Winter root mash** (pages 182 and 189)
MONDAY	**20-minute rice supper** (page 62)
TUESDAY	**Hot smoked mackerel jackets** (page 62)
WEDNESDAY	**Sweet chilli bangers** (page 110)
THURSDAY	**Rich tomato soup with pesto** (page 148)
FRIDAY	**Five-a-day tagine** (page 18)

Checklist
- This week the bulk of the budget goes on the roast lamb.
- Jacket potatoes are given a cheap but interesting filling.
- You can always have tomato soup whatever the season if you have sundried ones in your storecupboard.

plan 10

SATURDAY	**Spicy root and lentil casserole** (page 19)
SUNDAY	**Lamb shanks with chickpeas** (page 178)
MONDAY	**Sausage and tomato pasta** (page 105)
TUESDAY	**Chunky minestrone** (page 55)
WEDNESDAY	**Sweet potato and pineapple korma** (page 143)
THURSDAY	**Spicy bubble and squeak** (page 55)
FRIDAY	**Spicy root and lentil casserole** (page 19)

Checklist
- To balance the cost of the lamb shanks, lentils provide a cheap and useful source of protein.
- Spicy bubble and squeak is good on its own or is great with bacon or leftover sausages.
- Keeping a stock of different carbohydrates, such as pasta, rice and couscous, means you can enjoy a variety of textures and flavours all week (they don't cost a lot either).

Checklist

■ Risotto makes a good vegetarian menu for the weekend and is smart enough for guests.

■ Chicken is a perfect week-night roast as it doesn't take long to cook, and it provides some great leftovers for another meal.

■ This quick pasta dish or an egg-based recipe like these muffins are ideal meals if you are home late one night in the week.

SATURDAY	**Rösti bolognese bake** (page 27)
SUNDAY	**Tomato tarte Tatin, Leek and sage risotto** (pages 163 and 172)
MONDAY	**Fragrant roast chicken** (75)
TUESDAY	**Chicken and mushroom spud pies** (page 76)
WEDNESDAY	**20-minute seafood spaghetti** (page 105)
THURSDAY	**Scrambled egg muffin** (page 125)
FRIDAY	**Rösti bolognese bake** (page 27)

Checklist

■ Stewing beef is one of the most reasonably priced cuts and makes a filling meal. Make double, freeze half and defrost on Wednesday ready, to heat the next day.

■ Leftover cauliflower cheese becomes the topping for gammon steaks, which are cheap.

SATURDAY	**Potato focaccia Pugliese, Leek and sage risotto** (pages 202 and 172)
SUNDAY	**Hot beef stew with beans and peppers** (page 29)
MONDAY	**Cauliflower cheese** (page 59)
TUESDAY	**Mixed tuna and bean salad** (page 85)
WEDNESDAY	**Cheesy gammon grills** (page 59)
THURSDAY	**Hot beef stew with beans** (page 29)
FRIDAY	**Storecupboard corn pancakes** (page 125)

plan 13

SATURDAY	**Butternut squash casserole** (page 28)
SUNDAY	**Roast pork with pear sauce** (page 182)
MONDAY	**Good-for-you bolognese** (page 58)
TUESDAY	**Shepherd's pie jackets** (page 58)
WEDNESDAY	**Warm mushroom, lentil and goat's cheese salad** (page 86)
THURSDAY	**DIY kofta burgers** (page 132)
FRIDAY	**Butternut squash casserole** (page 28)

Checklist
■ The butternut squash casserole can be doubled up and frozen, ready for later in the week.
■ Kofta burgers are cheap and easy to make.

plan 14

SATURDAY	**Sausage and lentil simmer** (page 168)
SUNDAY	**Pan-fried chicken in mushroom sauce** (page 16)
MONDAY	**Tuna melt potato wedges** (page 124)
TUESDAY	**Oven-baked pepper risotto** (page 54)
WEDNESDAY	**Risotto cakes** (page 54)
THURSDAY	**Creamy egg curry** (page 96)
FRIDAY	**Pan-fried chicken in mushroom sauce** (page 16)

Checklist
■ Teaming more expensive cuts, like good-quality chicken, with a few veggie meals and an egg dish means that the week's shopping bill can still be within budget.
■ Make double of the chicken dish and put half in the freezer,. Don't forget to take it out of the freezer to defrost in the fridge on Thursday evening.

Checklist

■ Remember to take the second batch of Multi mince out of the freezer on Tuesday evening, ready to make the Spaghetti bolognese on Wednesday.

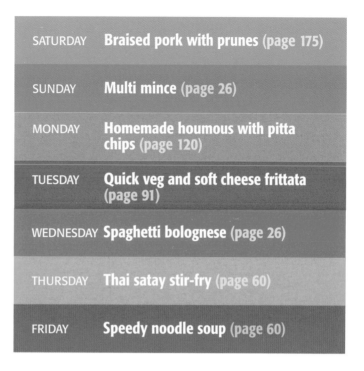

SATURDAY	**Braised pork with prunes** (page 175)	
SUNDAY	**Multi mince** (page 26)	
MONDAY	**Homemade houmous with pitta chips** (page 120)	
TUESDAY	**Quick veg and soft cheese frittata** (page 91)	
WEDNESDAY	**Spaghetti bolognese** (page 26)	
THURSDAY	**Thai satay stir-fry** (page 60)	
FRIDAY	**Speedy noodle soup** (page 60)	

plan 15

Checklist

■ Repeating dishes is good for the thrifty cook, as it makes the most of spices and ingredients that might otherwise hang about in the storecupboard.

SATURDAY	**Pan-fried chicken in mushroom sauce** (page 16)
SUNDAY	**Fresh lasagne with pesto** (page 169)
MONDAY	**Moroccan chickpea soup** (page 147)
TUESDAY	**20-minute rice supper** (page 62)
WEDNESDAY	**Hot smoked mackerel jackets** (page 62)
THURSDAY	**Pan-fried chicken in mushroom sauce** (page 16)
FRIDAY	**Sausage and tomato pasta** (page 105)

plan 16

plan 17	
SATURDAY	**Greek roast lamb, Sponge pudding** (pages 182 and 192)
SUNDAY	**Cheesy leek and potato pie** (page 37)
MONDAY	**Pizza Margherita** (page 128)
TUESDAY	**Lemon linguine with ham** (page 106)
WEDNESDAY	**Cheesy leek and potato pie** (page 37)
THURSDAY	**Chicken biryani** (page 72)
FRIDAY	**Coronation chicken rice salad** (page 72)

Checklist

■ Pavlova is a show-off pud that is incredibly cheap and easy to make. Use the leftover yolks for thickening sauces; they can also be frozen.

■ A plate pie, like the cheesy one here, is economical, and as you need no special dishes, it's easy to make another one to freeze. Defrost the night before as the plate won't be ovenproof straight from the freezer.

plan 18	
SATURDAY	**Tomato soup** (page 44)
SUNDAY	**Hot-smoked salmon salad, Spinach and green bean salad** (pages 164 and 184)
MONDAY	**Spanish spinach omelette** (page 63)
TUESDAY	**Omelette sandwiches** (page 63)
WEDNESDAY	**Coriander cod with carrot pilaf** (page 88)
THURSDAY	**Mozzarella, ham and pesto pizzas** (page 131)
FRIDAY	**Tomato soup** (page 44)

Checklist

■ Over-ripe bananas that didn't get eaten during the week make a tasty banana cake for the weekend.

■ There's no need to defrost the soup, as long as you heat it gently.

■ Any leftover salad from Sunday's salmon goes brilliantly with the omelette dish the next day.

Checklist

■ The meatloaf is an inexpensive weekend meal; make one and cook it, then you'll have leftovers for the week. Alternatively, make two and pop one in the freezer. Defrost it thoroughly before you cook it.

■ The pasta is a great Friday-night supper if you have friends coming over.

SATURDAY	**Meatloaf** (page 36)
SUNDAY	**Spinach roulade, Roast pears in red wine** (pages 171 and 195)
MONDAY	**Meatloaf** (page 36)
TUESDAY	**Caraway roast carrot and feta salad** (page 71)
WEDNESDAY	**Tomato and feta pasta sauce** (page 71)
THURSDAY	**Fragrant lamb flatbreads** (page 133)
FRIDAY	**Creamy courgette lasagne** (page 106)

Checklist

■ In the summer, you can vary the flavourings of the pavlova topping, according to what you can find. Any berry will do.

■ The mince is enough for four but easily doubles to make the Rösti bolognese for another night.

SATURDAY	**Chilli prawn linguine, Raspberry ripple Pavlova** (pages 167 and 192)
SUNDAY	**Multi mince** (page 26)
MONDAY	**Broad bean pilaf** (page 144)
TUESDAY	**Boiled bacon with cabbage and carrots** (page 70)
WEDNESDAY	**Pan-fried salmon with tabbouleh** (page 91)
THURSDAY	**Ham and leek cobbler** (page 70)
FRIDAY	**Rösti bolognese bake** (page 27)

plan 21

SATURDAY	**Fish pie** (page 39)
SUNDAY	**Tomato granita, Buttery trout, Summer pudding** (pages 166, 158 and 193)
MONDAY	**Spanish spinach omelette** (page 63)
TUESDAY	**Omelette sandwiches** (page 63)
WEDNESDAY	**Fish pie** (page 39)
THURSDAY	**Red onion, feta and olive tart** (page 130)
FRIDAY	**Green garden veg pie** (page 98)

Checklist

■ Make two fish pies and serve with a big, fresh green salad in warmer weather. Freeze one and remove from the freezer the night before to defrost overnight.

■ Take the pastry out of the freezer the same day and it will be defrosted in time for making the tart on Thursday.

plan 22

SATURDAY	**Vegetarian lasagne** (page 22)
SUNDAY	**Buttery trout, Lemon-roasted new potatoes** (pages 166 and 186)
MONDAY	**Bacon and broccoli pasta** (page 98)
TUESDAY	**Spanish spinach omelette** (page 63)
WEDNESDAY	**Omelette sandwiches** (page 63)
THURSDAY	**Ham, artichoke and lemon pilaf** (page 144)
FRIDAY	**Veggie lasagne** (page 22)

Checklist

■ Make double portions of the lasagne, freeze half, then take from the freezer the night before you want to eat it.

■ The pasta dish is a great meal to have after the weekend when you may have spare rashers of bacon to use up.

■ Ciabatta rolls are useful to have in the freezer, and you can warm them before using, if you like.

Checklist

■ Make double quantities of Goulash and freeze half for later in the week.

■ Chorizo will keep for ages if unsliced or well wrapped, so store any leftover in the fridge to use the next week.

plan 23

SATURDAY	**Chilli prawn linguine** (page 167)
SUNDAY	**Goulash in a dash** (page 35)
MONDAY	**Fragrant roast chicken** (page 75)
TUESDAY	**Roast chicken wraps** (page 77)
WEDNESDAY	**Superhealthy salmon burgers** (page 93)
THURSDAY	**Leek, butter bean and chorizo gratin** (page 138)
FRIDAY	**Goulash in a dash** (page 35)

Checklist

■ Pumpkin curry is the perfect all-year-round vegetarian dinner party meal. Make with butternut squash when pumpkins aren't in season.

■ Make double quantities of the chicken casserole and freeze half. Take it out of the freezer to defrost on Tuesday night.

plan 24

SATURDAY	**Pumpkin curry with chickpeas and spinach** (page 174)
SUNDAY	**Chicken casserole with red wine, ham and peppers** (page 30)
MONDAY	**Warm stilton salad** (page 64)
TUESDAY	**Creamy mushroom spaghetti** (page 64)
WEDNESDAY	**Chicken casserole with red wine, ham and peppers** (page 30)
THURSDAY	**Spicy tomato baked eggs** (page 123)
FRIDAY	**Mexican tuna and bean salad** (page 85)

index

Picture and recipe credits
BBC *Good Food* magazine
and BBC Books would like to
thank the following people
for providing photos. While
every effort has been made
to trace and acknowledge all
photographers, we should like
to apologize should there be
any errors or omissions.

Marie-Louise Avery p188,
p195; Steve Baxter p31,
p48;John Bennett p17;
Martin Brigdale p179, p181;

Peter Cassidy p23, p28, p33,
p107, p136, p177; Jean
Cazals p37, p45, p65, p159,
p190; Ken Field p97, p126;
Dean Grennan p142; William
Lingwood p109; Gareth
Morgans p41, p61, p67, p68,
p86, p94, p100, p130, p166,
p199; David Munns p36,
p38, p57, p115, p129, p150,
p187; Myles New p43. P53,
p103, p111, p112, p134,
p139, p172, p186, p205;
Elisabeth Parsons p122,
p132, p161, p175, p194;

Michael Paul p131; Craig
Robertson p69; Roger Stowell
p87, p168; Sam Stowell p27,
p203; Yuki Sugiura p174;
Dawie Verwey p141; Simon
Walton p25, p40, p73, p185;
Cameron Watt p200, p202;
Philip Webb p14, p34, p114,
p140, p147, p152, p165,
p170, p180, p183, p192,
p197; Simon Wheeler p21,
p56, p137, p169, p173,
p184; Kate Whitaker p13,
p66; Tim Young p121

All the recipes in this book
were created by the editorial
team at *Good Food* and by
regular contributors to the
magazine.